SOUL
Winner's
Guide

Compiled by
Jack Countryman

D1522105

Thomas Nelson
Since 1798

NASHVILLE   DALLAS   MEXICO CITY   RIO DE JANEIRO

ISBN-13: 9781400318346
ISBN-SE: 9781400318353

Printed in the United States of America
11 12 13 14 DP 5 4 3 2 1
www.thomasnelson.com

The Great Commission

And Jesus came and spoke to them, saying, "All authority has been given to Me in heaven and on earth. Go therefore and make disciples of all the nations, baptizing them in the name of the Father and of the Son and of the Holy Spirit, teaching them to observe all things that I have commanded you; and lo, I am with you always, even to the end of the age." Amen.

—*Matthew 28:18–20*

❧ Contents ❧

ENDORSEMENTS

The *Soul Winner's Guide* is an excellent Scripture guide to equip you as you become involved in evangelism. The Scriptural answers to overcoming difficult questions will prepare you to lead those who may be seeking to accept Christ as their personal savior. I strongly recommend this guide to anyone who desires to become a soul winner and to fulfill the Great Commission.

Dr. Johnny Hunt
Senior Pastor, First Baptist Church
Woodstock, GA

Jack Countryman is passionate about the world knowing Christ. From his heart and with his expertise, he has provided a resource for all Christ-followers. The *Soul Winner's Guide* is basic, helpful, and motivating. It will help you win your friends to Jesus Christ. It will assist your church in reaching the world. I strongly suggest that you get it for yourself and tell your church about it. We must finish the task together.

Dr. Ronnie W. Floyd
Senior Pastor, Cross Church
Northwest Arkansas

The *Soul Winner's Guide* is an outstanding resource to equip us to help people understand God's love and plan for their lives. The Word of God is always the key to understanding the freedom we have in Christ. We will be using this helpful, indexed guide through Scripture to assist our congregation with reaching those we are called to impact with the love and message of Jesus Christ.

Dr. Tom Mullins
Founding Pastor, Christ Fellowship Church
Palm Beach Gardens, FL

The *Soul Winner's Guide* is an outstanding resource for anyone who's serious about Christ's Great Commission. Jack Countryman shares a simple plan of salvation and a helpful collection of Scripture dealing with life's difficult questions and God's unfailing promises. A great tool for equipping us to share the Good News. I look forward to using it.

Bryant Wright
Senior Pastor, Johnson Ferry Baptist Church, Marietta, GA
President of the Southern Baptist Convention

Early in my ministry, I made a commitment to win 200 people to Christ each year—if at all possible. I set that goal and came close—winning 187 in a year and that was in face-to-face meetings. When I was asked a question I could not answer, I promised I would get back to the person with an answer. Over time, I learned the answer to most of the questions a person would ask. The *Soul Winner's Guide* is the perfect tool for anyone involved in winning someone to Christ. The questions you might be asked are answered Scripturally and this will prepare you to be the soul winner God wants you to be.

John Maxwell
Speaker, Best-Selling Author, Pastor

My mentor, Adrian Rogers, used to say, "if you are not winning people to Jesus Christ, you are not right with God." For those who aspire to follow Christ who "came to seek and to save that which was lost." Jack Countryman has provided a valuable tool that will be both powerful and productive. User friendly; Scripturally based; exhaustively researched—a great addition to the soul-winner's arsenal that I intend to carry with me as an aid to sharing the gospel.

Dr. James Merritt
Pastor, Cross Pointe Church, Duluth, GA

Scriptures to Answer People's
~ Excuses and Difficulties ~

Accountability of the believer.

But if we walk in the light as He is in the light, we have fellowship with one another, and the blood of Jesus Christ His Son cleanses us from all sin. If we say that we have no sin, we deceive ourselves, and the truth is not in us. If we confess our sins, He is faithful and just to forgive us our sins and to cleanse us from all unrighteousness. *1 John 1:7–9*

For we must all appear before the judgment seat of Christ, that each one may receive the things done in the body, according to what he has done, whether good or bad. Knowing, therefore, the terror of the Lord, we persuade men; but we are well known to God, and I also trust are well known in your consciences. *2 Corinthians 5:10–11*

My little children, these things I write to you, so that you may not sin. And if anyone sins, we have an Advocate with the Father, Jesus Christ the righteous. And He Himself is the propitiation for our sins, and not for ours only but also for the whole world. *1 John 2:1–2*

Afraid I cannot live it.

Now to Him who is able to keep you from stumbling, and to present you faultless before the presence of His glory with exceeding joy. *Jude 24*

Being confident of this very thing, that He who has begun a good work in you will complete it until the day of Jesus Christ.   *Philippians 1:6*

I have been crucified with Christ; it is no longer I who live, but Christ lives in me; and the life which I now live in the flesh I live by faith in the Son of God, who loved me and gave Himself for me.   *Galatians 2:20*

Always have been a Christian.

Behold, I was brought forth in iniquity, and in sin my mother conceived me.   *Psalm 51:5*

But as many as received Him, to them He gave the right to become children of God, to those who believe in His name.   *John 1:12*

Jesus answered and said to him, "Most assuredly, I say to you, unless one is born again, he cannot see the kingdom of God."   *John 3:3*

Amusements (worldly).

Do not love the world or the things in the world. If anyone loves the world, the love of the Father is not in him. For all that is in the world—the lust of the flesh, the lust of the eyes, and the pride of life—is not of the Father but is of the world. And the world is passing away, and the lust of it; but he who does the will of God abides forever.

1 John 2:15–17

Therefore, whether you eat or drink, or whatever you do, do all to the glory of God.   *1 Corinthians 10:31*

Abstain from every form of evil.   *1 Thessalonians 5:22*

Believer who will not repent.

Do not be deceived, God is not mocked; for whatever a man sows, that he will also reap. For he who sows to his flesh will of the flesh reap corruption, but he who sows to the Spirit will of the Spirit reap everlasting life.
Galatians 6:7–8

"For whom the Lord loves He chastens, and scourges every son whom He receives."   *Hebrews 12:6*

For this reason many are weak and sick among you, and many sleep.   *1 Corinthians 11:30*

Bible is the Word of God.

For prophecy never came by the will of man, but holy men of God spoke as they were moved by the Holy Spirit.
2 Peter 1:21

All Scripture is given by inspiration of God, and is profitable for doctrine, for reproof, for correction, for instruction in righteousness.   *2 Timothy 3:16*

For this reason we also thank God without ceasing, because when you received the word of God which you heard from us, you welcomed it not as the word of men, but as it is in truth, the word of God, which also effectively works in you who believe. *1 Thessalonians 2:13*

Cannot believe.

But without faith it is impossible to please Him, for he who comes to God must believe that He is, and that He is a rewarder of those who diligently seek Him. *Hebrews 11:6*

"But the cowardly, unbelieving, abominable, murderers, sexually immoral, sorcerers, idolaters, and all liars shall have their part in the lake which burns with fire and brimstone, which is the second death." *Revelation 21:8*

Trust in the LORD with all your heart, and lean not on your own understanding; in all your ways acknowledge Him, and He shall direct your paths. *Proverbs 3:5–6*

Cannot forgive.

"'Should you not also have had compassion on your fellow servant, just as I had pity on you?' And his master was angry, and delivered him to the torturers until he should pay all that was due to him.

'So My heavenly Father also will do to you if each of you, from his heart, does not forgive his brother his trespasses.'" *Matthew 18:33–35*

"For if you forgive men their trespasses, your heavenly Father will also forgive you." *Matthew 6:14*

And be kind to one another, tenderhearted, forgiving one another, even as God in Christ forgave you.
Ephesians 4:32

Cannot give up my friends.

Adulterers and adulteresses! Do you not know that friendship with the world is enmity with God? Whoever therefore wants to be a friend of the world makes himself an enemy of God. *James 4:4*

And God both raised up the Lord and will also raise us up by His power. Do you not know that your bodies are members of Christ? Shall I then take the members of Christ and make them members of a harlot? Certainly not! Or do you not know that he who is joined to a harlot is one body with her? For "the two," He says, "shall become one flesh." But he who is joined to the Lord is one spirit with Him. Flee sexual immorality. Every sin that a man does is outside the body, but he who commits sexual immorality sins against his own body. *1 Corinthians 6:14–18*

Do not be envious of evil men, nor desire to be with them. *Proverbs 24:1*

Cannot understand the Bible.

But even if our gospel is veiled, it is veiled to those who are perishing. *2 Corinthians 4:3*

But the natural man does not receive the things of the Spirit of God, for they are foolishness to him; nor can he know them, because they are spiritually discerned.

1 Corinthians 2:14

But their minds were blinded. For until this day the same veil remains unlifted in the reading of the Old Testament, because the veil is taken away in Christ. But even to this day, when Moses is read, a veil lies on their heart. Nevertheless when one turns to the Lord, the veil is taken away. *2 Corinthians 3:14–16*

Church, do not have to attend.

Not forsaking the assembling of ourselves together, as is the manner of some, but exhorting one another, and so much the more as you see the Day approaching.

Hebrews 10:25

So continuing daily with one accord in the temple, and breaking bread from house to house, they ate their food with gladness and simplicity of heart. *Acts 2:46*

But do you want to know, O foolish man, that faith without works is dead? *James 2:20*

Church member.

Jesus answered and said to him, "Most assuredly, I say to you, unless one is born again, he cannot see the kingdom of God." *John 3:3*

Jesus said to him, "I am the way, the truth, and the life. No one comes to the Father except through Me." John 14:6

And this is the testimony: that God has given us eternal life, and this life is in His Son. He who has the Son has life; he who does not have the Son of God does not have life.

1 John 5:11–12

Death ends everything.

And as it is appointed for men to die once, but after this the judgment.... *Hebrews 9:27*

"There was a certain rich man who was clothed in purple and fine linen and fared sumptuously every day. But there was a certain beggar named Lazarus, full of sores, who was laid at his gate, desiring to be fed with the crumbs which fell from the rich man's table. Moreover the dogs came and licked his sores. So it was that the beggar died, and was carried by the angels to Abraham's bosom. The rich man also died and was buried. And being in torments in Hades, he lifted up his eyes and saw Abraham afar off, and Lazarus in his bosom.

"Then he cried and said, 'Father Abraham, have mercy on me, and send Lazarus that he may dip the tip of his finger in water and cool my tongue; for I am tormented in this flame.'" *Luke 16:19–24*

Then I saw a great white throne and Him who sat on it, from whose face the earth and the heaven fled away. And there was found no place for them. And I saw the dead, small and great, standing before God, and books were opened. And another book was opened, which is the Book of Life. And the dead were judged according to their works, by the things which were written in the books. The sea gave up the dead who were in it, and Death and Hades delivered up the dead who were in them. And they were judged, each one according to his works. Then Death and Hades were cast into the lake of fire. This is the second death. And anyone not found written in the Book of Life was cast into the lake of fire.   *Revelation 20:11–15*

Everyone will go to heaven.

"He who believes in the Son has everlasting life; and he who does not believe the Son shall not see life, but the wrath of God abides on him."   *John 3:36*

"He who believes and is baptized will be saved; but he who does not believe will be condemned."   *Mark 16:16*

That they all may be condemned who did not believe the truth but had pleasure in unrighteousness.
2 Thessalonians 2:12

Feeling, do not feel ready.

For by grace you have been saved through faith, and that not of yourselves; it is the gift of God, not of works, lest anyone should boast.   *Ephesians 2:8–9*

"And the one who comes to Me I will by no means cast out."   *John 6:37*

And this is the testimony: that God has given us eternal life, and this life is in His Son. He who has the Son has life; he who does not have the Son of God does not have life.

1 John 5:11–12

God is too good to damn anyone.

For if God did not spare the angels who sinned, but cast them down to hell and delivered them into chains of darkness, to be reserved for judgment.   *2 Peter 2:4*

"He who believes and is baptized will be saved; but he who does not believe will be condemned."   *Mark 16:16*

That they all may be condemned who did not believe the truth but had pleasure in unrighteousness.

2 Thessalonians 2:12

God's existence.

Because what may be known of God is manifest in them, for God has shown it to them. For since the creation of the world His invisible attributes are clearly seen, being understood by the things that are made, even His eternal power and Godhead, so that they are without excuse.

Romans 1:19–20

The heavens declare the glory of God; and the firmament shows His handiwork.   *Psalm 19:1*

And without controversy great is the mystery of godliness: God was manifested in the flesh, justified in the Spirit, seen by angels, preached among the Gentiles, believed on in the world, received up in glory.

1 Timothy 3:16

How do we know there is a heaven?

"In this manner, therefore, pray: Our Father in heaven, hallowed be Your name."   *Matthew 6:9*

For we know that if our earthly house, this tent, is destroyed, we have a building from God, a house not made with hands, eternal in the heavens.   *2 Corinthians 5:1*

Now I saw a new heaven and a new earth, for the first heaven and the first earth had passed away. Also there was no more sea. Then I, John, saw the holy city, New Jerusalem, coming down out of heaven from God, prepared as a bride adorned for her husband. And I heard a loud voice from heaven saying, "Behold, the tabernacle of God is with men, and He will dwell with them, and they shall be His people. God Himself will be with them and be their God. And God will wipe away every tear from their eyes; there shall be no more death, nor sorrow, nor crying. There shall be no more pain, for the former things have passed away."

Revelation 21:1–4

How do we know there is a hell?

"There was a certain rich man who was clothed in purple and fine linen and fared sumptuously every day.

But there was a certain beggar named Lazarus, full of sores, who was laid at his gate, desiring to be fed with the crumbs which fell from the rich man's table. Moreover the dogs came and licked his sores. So it was that the beggar died, and was carried by the angels to Abraham's bosom. The rich man also died and was buried. And being in torments in Hades, he lifted up his eyes and saw Abraham afar off, and Lazarus in his bosom.

"Then he cried and said, 'Father Abraham, have mercy on me, and send Lazarus that he may dip the tip of his finger in water and cool my tongue; for I am tormented in this flame.'"   *Luke 16:19–24*

"Then He will also say to those on the left hand, 'Depart from Me, you cursed, into the everlasting fire prepared for the devil and his angels.'"   *Matthew 25:41*

"But I will show you whom you should fear: Fear Him who, after He has killed, has power to cast into hell; yes, I say to you, fear Him!"   *Luke 12:5*

Hypocrites, too many.

So then each of us shall give account of himself to God.
                                                          Romans 14:12

"And will cut him in two and appoint him his portion with the hypocrites. There shall be weeping and gnashing of teeth."   *Matthew 24:51*

And whatever you do, do it heartily, as to the Lord and not to men.   *Colossians 3:23*

11

I pray every day.

Jesus answered and said to him, "Most assuredly, I say to you, unless one is born again, he cannot see the kingdom of God."   *John 3:3*

But as many as received Him, to them He gave the right to become children of God, to those who believe in His name.   *John 1:12*

"Behold, I stand at the door and knock. If anyone hears My voice and opens the door, I will come in to him and dine with him, and he with Me."   *Revelation 3:20*

Jehovah's Witnesses.

Jesus answered and said to him, "Most assuredly, I say to you, unless one is born again, he cannot see the kingdom of God."   *John 3:3*

For by grace you have been saved through faith, and that not of yourselves; it is the gift of God, not of works, lest anyone should boast.   *Ephesians 2:8–9*

And we know that the Son of God has come and has given us an understanding, that we may know Him who is true; and we are in Him who is true, in His Son Jesus Christ. This is the true God and eternal life.   *1 John 5:20*

Jewish people.

All we like sheep have gone astray; we have turned, every one, to his own way; and the LORD has laid on Him the iniquity of us all. *Isaiah 53:6*

Jesus answered and said to him, "Most assuredly, I say to you, unless one is born again, he cannot see the kingdom of God." *John 3:3*

"And as Moses lifted up the serpent in the wilderness, even so must the Son of Man be lifted up, that whoever believes in Him should not perish but have eternal life. For God so loved the world that He gave His only begotten Son, that whoever believes in Him should not perish but have everlasting life. For God did not send His Son into the world to condemn the world, but that the world through Him might be saved. He who believes in Him is not condemned; but he who does not believe is condemned already, because he has not believed in the name of the only begotten Son of God." *John 3:14–18*

Mormonism.

Jesus answered and said to him, "Most assuredly, I say to you, unless one is born again, he cannot see the kingdom of God." *John 3:3*

For by grace you have been saved through faith, and that not of yourselves; it is the gift of God, not of works, lest anyone should boast. *Ephesians 2:8–9*

"Knowing that a man is not justified by the works of the law but by faith in Jesus Christ, even we have believed in Christ Jesus, that we might be justified by faith in Christ and not by the works of the law; for by the works of the law no flesh shall be justified."   *Galatians 2:16*

Must get better first.

"The one who comes to Me I will by no means cast out."   *John 6:37*

"Come now, and let us reason together," says the LORD, "Though your sins are like scarlet, they shall be as white as snow; though they are red like crimson, they shall be as wool."   *Isaiah 1:18*

"And the tax collector, standing afar off, would not so much as raise his eyes to heaven, but beat his breast, saying, 'God, be merciful to me a sinner!' I tell you, this man went down to his house justified rather than the other; for everyone who exalts himself will be humbled, and he who humbles himself will be exalted."   *Luke 18:13–14*

Not now.

For He says: "In an acceptable time I have heard you, and in the day of salvation I have helped you." Behold, now is the accepted time; behold, now is the day of salvation.   *2 Corinthians 6:2*

Do not boast about tomorrow, for you do not know what a day may bring forth.

Proverbs 27:1

And the Lord said, "My Spirit shall not strive with man forever."

Genesis 6:3

Not willing to give up my sin.

That they all may be condemned who did not believe the truth but had pleasure in unrighteousness.

2 Thessalonians 2:12

Do not be deceived, God is not mocked; for whatever a man sows, that he will also reap. For he who sows to his flesh will of the flesh reap corruption, but he who sows to the Spirit will of the Spirit reap everlasting life.

Galatians 6:7–8

Then, when desire has conceived, it gives birth to sin; and sin, when it is full grown, brings forth death.

James 1:15

Other religions.

Jesus answered and said to him, "Most assuredly, I say to you, unless one is born again, he cannot see the kingdom of God."

John 3:3

Jesus said to him, "I am the way, the truth, and the life. No one comes to the Father except through Me." *John 14:6*

For there is one God and one Mediator between God and men, the Man Christ Jesus.

1 Timothy 2:5

Perscution, fear of.

"Blessed are you when they revile and persecute you, and say all kinds of evil against you falsely for My sake. Rejoice and be exceedingly glad, for great is your reward in heaven, for so they persecuted the prophets who were before you."

Matthew 5:11–12

For I consider that the sufferings of this present time are not worthy to be compared with the glory which shall be revealed in us.

Romans 8:18

If we endure, we shall also reign with Him.

2 Timothy 2:12

Procrastination.

For He says: "In an acceptable time I have heard you, and in the day of salvation I have helped you." Behold, now is the accepted time; behold, now is the day of salvation.

2 Corinthians 6:2

My son, be wise, and make my heart glad, that I may answer him who reproaches me.

Proverbs 27:11

And the LORD said, "My Spirit shall not strive with man forever."

Genesis 6:3

Self-righteousness.

Also He spoke this parable to some who trusted in themselves that they were righteous, and despised others: "Two men went up to the temple to pray, one a Pharisee and the other a tax collector. The Pharisee stood and prayed thus with himself, 'God, I thank You that I am not like other men—extortioners, unjust, adulterers, or even as this tax collector. I fast twice a week; I give tithes of all that I possess.' And the tax collector, standing afar off, would not so much as raise his eyes to heaven, but beat his breast, saying, 'God, be merciful to me a sinner!' I tell you, this man went down to his house justified rather than the other; for everyone who exalts himself will be humbled, and he who humbles himself will be exalted."

Luke 18:9–14

For by grace you have been saved through faith, and that not of yourselves; it is the gift of God, not of works, lest anyone should boast. *Ephesians 2:8–9*

Not by works of righteousness which we have done, but according to His mercy He saved us, through the washing of regeneration and renewing of the Holy Spirit. *Titus 3:5*

Sincerity is all that matters.

There is a way that seems right to a man, but its end is the way of death. *Proverbs 14:12*

Jesus said to him, "I am the way, the truth, and the life. No one comes to the Father except through Me." *John 14:6*

17

But as many as received Him, to them He gave the right to become children of God, to those who believe in His name. *John 1:12*

Spiritism.

Now the works of the flesh are evident, which are: adultery, fornication, uncleanness, lewdness, idolatry, sorcery, hatred, contentions, jealousies, outbursts of wrath, selfish ambitions, dissensions, heresies, envy, murders, drunkenness, revelries, and the like; of which I tell you beforehand, just as I also told you in time past, that those who practice such things will not inherit the kingdom of God. *Galatians 5:19–21*

"But the cowardly, unbelieving, abominable, murderers, sexually immoral, sorcerers, idolaters, and all liars shall have their part in the lake which burns with fire and brimstone, which is the second death." *Revelation 21:8*

"And the person who turns to mediums and familiar spirits, to prostitute himself with them, I will set My face against that person and cut him off from his people." *Leviticus 20:6*

Too great a sinner.

Therefore He is also able to save to the uttermost those who come to God through Him, since He always lives to make intercession for them. *Hebrews 7:25*

"The one who comes to Me I will by no means cast out."

John 6:37

"The blood of Jesus Christ His Son cleanses us from all sin."

1 John 1:7

Too much to give up.

"For what will it profit a man if he gains the whole world, and loses his own soul? Or what will a man give in exchange for his soul?"

Mark 8:36–37

"But seek first the kingdom of God and His righteousness, and all these things shall be added to you."

Matthew 6:33

Do not love the world or the things in the world. If anyone loves the world, the love of the Father is not in him. For all that is in the world—the lust of the flesh, the lust of the eyes, and the pride of life—is not of the Father but is of the world. And the world is passing away, and the lust of it; but he who does the will of God abides forever.

1 John 2:15–17

Trying to go to heaven.

Jesus said to him, "I am the way, the truth, and the life. No one comes to the Father except through Me." *John 14:6*

For by grace you have been saved through faith, and that not of yourselves; it is the gift of God, not of works, lest anyone should boast.

Ephesians 2:8–9

"Knowing that a man is not justified by the works of the law but by faith in Jesus Christ, even we have believed in Christ Jesus, that we might be justified by faith in Christ and not by the works of the law; for by the works of the law no flesh shall be justified. *Galatians 2:16*

Unpardonable sin.

"Therefore I say to you, every sin and blasphemy will be forgiven men, but the blasphemy against the Spirit will not be forgiven men. Anyone who speaks a word against the Son of Man, it will be forgiven him; but whoever speaks against the Holy Spirit, it will not be forgiven him, either in this age or in the age to come." *Matthew 12:31–32*

"The one who comes to Me I will by no means cast out." *John 6:37*

For "whoever calls on the name of the LORD shall be saved." *Romans 10:13*

When God wants me saved, He will let me know.

For He says: "In an acceptable time I have heard you, and in the day of salvation I have helped you." Behold, now is the accepted time; behold, now is the day of salvation. *2 Corinthians 6:2*

"The heart is deceitful above all things, and desperately wicked; who can know it?" *Jeremiah 17:9*

"Come now, and let us reason together," says the LORD, "Though your sins are like scarlet, they shall be as white as snow; though they are red like crimson, they shall be as wool."   *Isaiah 1:18*

Where I spend eternity is up to God.

But as many as received Him, to them He gave the right to become children of God, to those who believe in His name.   *John 1:12*

"And if it seems evil to you to serve the LORD, choose for yourselves this day whom you will serve, whether the gods which your fathers served that were on the other side of the River, or the gods of the Amorites, in whose land you dwell. But as for me and my house, we will serve the LORD."   *Joshua 24:15*

There is a way that seems right to a man, but its end is the way of death.   *Proverbs 14:12*

Works will take me to heaven.

For by grace you have been saved through faith, and that not of yourselves; it is the gift of God, not of works, lest anyone should boast.   *Ephesians 2:8–9*

Not by works of righteousness which we have done, but according to His mercy He saved us, through the washing of regeneration and renewing of the Holy Spirit.   *Titus 3:5*

"Knowing that a man is not justified by the works of the law but by faith in Jesus Christ, even we have believed in Christ Jesus, that we might be justified by faith in Christ and not by the works of the law; for by the works of the law no flesh shall be justified. *Galatians 2:16*

For the law was given through Moses, but grace and truth came through Jesus Christ. *John 1:17*

I commend you to God and to the word of His grace, which is able to build you up and give you an inheritance among all those who are sanctified. *Acts 20:32*

✨ God's Plan of Salvation ✨
Preface

"God so loved the world that He gave His only begotten Son,
that whoever believes in Him should not perish
but have everlasting life."

—*John 3:16*

John 3:16 is one of the most well-known Scripture verses throughout the world. As Max Lucado states, "It's the Hope Diamond of the Bible."

The Bible is the greatest book that has ever been written. In it God Himself speaks to humankind. The Bible is not simply one book. It is an entire library of books covering the whole range of literature. It includes history, poetry, drama, biography, prophecy, philosophy, science, and inspirational reading. How do you know the Bible is true? God declares in Isaiah 46:9–10: "Remember the former things of old, for I am God, and there is no other; I am God, and there is none like Me, declaring the end from the beginning, and from ancient times things that are not yet done, saying, 'My counsel shall stand, and I will do all My pleasure.'"

As D. James Kennedy revealed in his book *Why I Believe*:

> The prophecies of the Bible are incredibly specific and detailed. They must be exactly fulfilled. The prophecies cannot possibly be just good guesses because they concerned themselves with things that had no likelihood of ever coming to pass. They predicted the very opposite

of the natural expectations of human beings. They could not have been written after the events and pawned off as prophecies, because in hundreds of instances the fulfillment of the prophecy did not take place until hundreds of years after the death of the prophets. In all the writings of Buddha, Confucius, and Lao-tse, you will not find a single example of predicted prophecy. In the Koran (the writings of Mohammed) there is one instance of a specific prophecy—a self-fulfilling prophecy—that he, Mohammed, would return to Mecca, quite different from the Old Testament prophecies about Jesus and the prophecy of Jesus, where He said that He would return from the grave. One is easily fulfilled by man's own choice, and the other is impossible for any human being.

The Bible is divided into two sections: The Old Testament covers the creation of man, the fall of man, and reveals God's plan of redemption for man through Christ. The New Testament covers the time of Christ's birth, life, death, resurrection, ascension to heaven, and His ultimate return to earth. While on earth, God revealed Himself through Jesus Christ as evidenced in John 14:9, where Jesus said, "Have I been with you so long, and yet you have not known Me, Philip? He who has seen Me has seen the Father." Colossians 2:9 declares, "For in Him dwells all the fullness of the Godhead bodily."

The Bible alone truly can answer the greatest questions that humankind throughout the ages has asked:

"*Where have I come from?*"
"*Where am I going?*"
"*Why am I here?*"

"How can I know the truth?"

The Bible alone reveals the truth about God, explains the origin of man, points out the only way to know God and how to live in His presence both now and for eternity.

The New Testament reveals God through Christ's life. We learn that we are greatly loved by God and that God is righteous and holy and will not tolerate sin. That is why, in His great love for us, God chose to send His Son to take our place of punishment. Romans 5:8 says, "God demonstrates His own love toward us, in that while we were *still sinners, Christ died* for us" (emphasis added).

Jesus said, "I am the way, the truth, and the life. No one comes to the Father except through Me" (John 14:6).

We learn in the Bible, "If you confess with your mouth the Lord Jesus and believe in your heart that God has raised Him from the dead, you will be saved. For with the heart one believes unto righteousness, and with the mouth confession is made unto salvation" (Romans 10:9–10).

Also, Jesus Himself reveals to us through the scriptures: "I have come that they may have life, and that they may have it more abundantly" (John 10:10).

Can you imagine someone loving you so much that he would die for you? The New Testament continues to reveal God's love for us in Romans 8:38–39: "Neither death nor life, nor angels nor principalities nor powers, nor things present nor things to come, nor height nor depth, nor any other created thing, shall be able to separate us from the love of God which is in Christ Jesus our Lord."

The Bible is God's story of His amazing love for you—a love so profound and so intentional that "He gave His only begotten Son, that whoever believes in Him should not perish but have everlasting life" (John 3:16).

Jesus says, "Behold, I stand at the door and knock. If anyone hears My voice and opens the door, I will come in to him and dine with him, and he with Me" (Revelation 3:20).

Accept God's free gift of salvation. You can't earn it, you can't perform for it or ever be good enough for it, but you can receive it because God chooses to give it to you.

Ephesians 2:8–9 reveals: "For by grace you have been saved through faith, and that not of yourselves; it is the gift of God, not of works, lest anyone should boast." And then in John 1:12–13 we learn, "But as many as received Him, to them He gave the right to become children of God, to those who believe in His name: who were born, not of blood, nor of the will of the flesh, nor of the will of man, but of God."

Begin the most amazing journey of your life that will continue throughout eternity! Go to God in prayer; confess that you are a sinner who needs God's AMAZING GRACE; that you believe Jesus is the Son of God; that He died on the cross for you; and that you desire the abundant, eternal, intimate fellowship with Him that He promises to give when you believe.

❧ God's Plan of Salvation ❧

Therefore, just as through one man sin entered the world, and death through sin, and thus death spread to all men, because all sinned.   *Romans 5:12*

For all have sinned and fall short of the glory of God, being justified freely by His grace through the redemption that is in Christ Jesus.   *Romans 3:23–24*

For the wages of sin is death, but the gift of God is eternal life in Christ Jesus our Lord.   *Romans 6:23*

But God demonstrates His own love toward us, in that while we were still sinners, Christ died for us.   *Romans 5:8*

Moreover, brethren, I declare to you the gospel which I preached to you, which also you received and in which you stand, by which also you are saved, if you hold fast that word which I preached to you—unless you believed in vain. For I delivered to you first of all that which I also received: that Christ died for our sins according to the Scriptures, and that He was buried, and that He rose again the third day according to the Scriptures.

1 Corinthians 15:1–4

"For God did not send His Son into the world to condemn the world, but that the world through Him might be saved."   *John 3:17*

"He who believes in the Son has everlasting life; and he who does not believe the Son shall not see life, but the wrath of God abides on him." *John 3:36*

"For God so loved the world that He gave His only begotten Son, that whoever believes in Him should not perish but have everlasting life." *John 3:16*

But as many as received Him, to them He gave the right to become children of God, to those who believe in His name. *John 1:12*

For by grace you have been saved through faith, and that not of yourselves; it is the gift of God, not of works, lest anyone should boast. *Ephesians 2:8–9*

"Behold, I stand at the door and knock. If anyone hears My voice and opens the door, I will come in to him and dine with him, and he with Me." *Revelation 3:20*

But what does it say? "The word is near you, in your mouth and in your heart" (that is, the word of faith which we preach): that if you confess with your mouth the Lord Jesus and believe in your heart that God has raised Him from the dead, you will be saved. For with the heart one believes unto righteousness, and with the mouth confession is made unto salvation. *Romans 10:8–10*

"Therefore whoever confesses Me before men, him I will also confess before My Father who is in heaven." *Matthew 10:32*

And this is the testimony: that God has given us eternal life, and this life is in His Son. He who has the Son has life; he who does not have the Son of God does not have life. These things I have written to you who believe in the name of the Son of God, that you may know that you have eternal life, and that you may continue to believe in the name of the Son of God. *1 John 5:11–13*

❧ GOD'S PROMISES ❧
FOR YOUR EVERY NEED

JESUS IS YOUR—Lord.

Therefore God also has highly exalted Him and given Him the name which is above every name, that at the name of Jesus every knee should bow, of those in heaven, and of those on earth, and of those under the earth, and that every tongue should confess that Jesus Christ is Lord, to the glory of God the Father.   *Philippians 2:9–11*

That if you confess with your mouth the Lord Jesus and believe in your heart that God has raised Him from the dead, you will be saved. For with the heart one believes unto righteousness, and with the mouth confession is made unto salvation.   *Romans 10:9–10*

"But why do you call Me 'Lord, Lord,' and not do the things which I say?"   *Luke 6:46*

And do not present your members as instruments of unrighteousness to sin, but present yourselves to God as being alive from the dead, and your members as instruments of righteousness to God. For sin shall not have dominion over you, for you are not under law but under grace.

What then? Shall we sin because we are not under law but under grace? Certainly not! Do you not know that to whom you present yourselves slaves to obey, you are that one's slaves whom you obey, whether of sin leading to death, or of obedience leading to righteousness?

Romans 6:13–16

I beseech you therefore, brethren, by the mercies of God, that you present your bodies a living sacrifice, holy, acceptable to God, which is your reasonable service. And do not be conformed to this world, but be transformed by the renewing of your mind, that you may prove what is that good and acceptable and perfect will of God.

Romans 12:1–2

Or do you not know that your body is the temple of the Holy Spirit who is in you, whom you have from God, and you are not your own? For you were bought at a price; therefore glorify God in your body and in your spirit, which are God's.

1 Corinthians 6:19–20

"Therefore let all the house of Israel know assuredly that God has made this Jesus, whom you crucified, both Lord and Christ."

Acts 2:36

For if we live, we live to the Lord; and if we die, we die to the Lord. Therefore, whether we live or die, we are the Lord's.

Romans 14:8

Blessed be the Lord, who daily loads us with benefits, the God of our salvation!

Psalm 68:19

But it is good for me to draw near to God; I have put my trust in the Lord GOD, that I may declare all Your works.

Psalm 73:28

For You, Lord, are good, and ready to forgive, and abundant in mercy to all those who call upon You.   *Psalm 86:5*

"For the Lord God will help Me; therefore I will not be disgraced; therefore I have set My face like a flint, and I know that I will not be ashamed."   *Isaiah 50:7*

"'And you shall love the Lord your God with all your heart, with all your soul, with all your mind, and with all your strength.' This is the first commandment." *Mark 12:30*

"For David says concerning Him: 'I foresaw the Lord always before my face, for He is at my right hand, that I may not be shaken.'"   *Acts 2:25*

JESUS IS YOUR—Love.

But God demonstrates His own love toward us, in that while we were still sinners, Christ died for us.   *Romans 5:8*

"For God so loved the world that He gave His only begotten Son, that whoever believes in Him should not perish but have everlasting life."   *John 3:16*

Beloved, let us love one another, for love is of God; and everyone who loves is born of God and knows God. He who does not love does not know God, for God is love. In this the love of God was manifested toward us, that God has sent His only begotten Son into the world, that we might live through Him. In this is love, not that we loved God, but that He loved us and sent His Son to be the propitiation for our sins. Beloved, if God so loved us, we also ought to love one another.

No one has seen God at any time. If we love one another, God abides in us, and His love has been perfected in us.   *1 John 4:7–12*

And we have known and believed the love that God has for us. God is love, and he who abides in love abides in God, and God in him. . . . We love Him because He first loved us.

1 John 4:16, 19

"As the Father loved Me, I also have loved you; abide in My love. If you keep My commandments, you will abide in My love, just as I have kept My Father's commandments and abide in His love. These things I have spoken to you, that My joy may remain in you, and that your joy may be full. This is My commandment, that you love one another as I have loved you. Greater love has no one than this, than to lay down one's life for his friends. . . . These things I command you, that you love one another."

John 15:9–13, 17

That Christ may dwell in your hearts through faith; that you, being rooted and grounded in love, may be able to comprehend with all the saints what is the width and length and depth and height—to know the love of Christ which passes knowledge; that you may be filled with all the fullness of God.

Ephesians 3:17–19

I love those who love me, and those who seek me diligently will find me.

Proverbs 8:17

The Lord has appeared of old to me, saying: "Yes, I have loved you with an everlasting love; therefore with lovingkindness I have drawn you."

Jeremiah 31:3

I will betroth you to Me forever; yes, I will betroth you to Me in righteousness and justice, in lovingkindness and mercy. *Hosea 2:19*

"He who has My commandments and keeps them, it is he who loves Me. And he who loves Me will be loved by My Father, and I will love him and manifest Myself to him." *John 14:21*

The LORD will command His lovingkindness in the daytime, and in the night His song shall be with me—a prayer to the God of my life. *Psalm 42:8*

And now abide faith, hope, love, these three; but the greatest of these is love. *1 Corinthians 13:13*

For I am persuaded that neither death nor life, nor angels nor principalities nor powers, nor things present nor things to come, nor height nor depth, nor any other created thing, shall be able to separate us from the love of God which is in Christ Jesus our Lord. *Romans 8:38–39*

JESUS IS YOUR—Peace.

You will keep him in perfect peace, whose mind is stayed on You, because he trusts in You. *Isaiah 26:3*

But now in Christ Jesus you who once were far off have been brought near by the blood of Christ. For He Himself is our peace, who has made both one, and has broken down the middle wall of separation. *Ephesians 2:13–14*

For unto us a Child is born, unto us a Son is given; and the government will be upon His shoulder. And His name will be called Wonderful, Counselor, Mighty God, Everlasting Father, Prince of Peace. Of the increase of His government and peace there will be no end, upon the throne of David and over His kingdom, to order it and establish it with judgment and justice from that time forward, even forever. The zeal of the Lord of hosts will perform this.

Isaiah 9:6–7

And the God of peace will crush Satan under your feet shortly. The grace of our Lord Jesus Christ be with you. Amen. *Romans 16:20*

LORD, You will establish peace for us, for You have also done all our works in us. *Isaiah 26:12*

The things which you learned and received and heard and saw in me, these do, and the God of peace will be with you. *Philippians 4:9*

Therefore, having been justified by faith, we have peace with God through our Lord Jesus Christ. *Romans 5:1*

And let the peace of God rule in your hearts, to which also you were called in one body; and be thankful.

Colossians 3:15

I will both lie down in peace, and sleep; for You alone, O LORD, make me dwell in safety. *Psalm 4:8*

The LORD will give strength to His people; the LORD will bless His people with peace.   *Psalm 29:11*

"Peace I leave with you, My peace I give to you; not as the world gives do I give to you. Let not your heart be troubled, neither let it be afraid."   *John 14:27*

Be anxious for nothing, but in everything by prayer and supplication, with thanksgiving, let your requests be made known to God; and the peace of God, which surpasses all understanding, will guard your hearts and minds through Christ Jesus.   *Philippians 4:6–7*

JESUS IS YOUR—Forgiveness.

To the praise of the glory of His grace, by which He made us accepted in the Beloved. In Him we have redemption through His blood, the forgiveness of sins, according to the riches of His grace.   *Ephesians 1:6–7*

You have forgiven the iniquity of Your people; you have covered all their sin.   *Psalm 85:2*

Therefore, if anyone is in Christ, he is a new creation; old things have passed away; behold, all things have become new.   *2 Corinthians 5:17*

As far as the east is from the west, so far has He removed our transgressions from us.   *Psalm 103:12*

My little children, these things I write to you, so that you may not sin. And if anyone sins, we have an Advocate with the Father, Jesus Christ the righteous.   *1 John 2:1*

If we confess our sins, He is faithful and just to forgive us our sins and to cleanse us from all unrighteousness.
1 John 1:9

Bearing with one another, and forgiving one another, if anyone has a complaint against another; even as Christ forgave you, so you also must do.   *Colossians 3:13*

"And whenever you stand praying, if you have anything against anyone, forgive him, that your Father in heaven may also forgive you your trespasses."   *Mark 11:25*

And you, being dead in your trespasses and the uncircumcision of your flesh, He has made alive together with Him, having forgiven you all trespasses.   *Colossians 2:13*

I will cleanse them from all their iniquity by which they have sinned against Me, and I will pardon all their iniquities by which they have sinned and by which they have transgressed against Me.   *Jeremiah 33:8*

"For I will be merciful to their unrighteousness, and their sins and their lawless deeds I will remember no more."   *Hebrews 8:12*

"I, even I, am He who blots out your transgressions for My own sake; and I will not remember your sins."
Isaiah 43:25

Let the wicked forsake his way, and the unrighteous
man his thoughts; let him return to the LORD, and He
will have mercy on him; and to our God, for He will
abundantly pardon.   *Isaiah 55:7*

"Come now, and let us reason together," says the LORD,
"though your sins are like scarlet, they shall be as white as
snow; though they are red like crimson, they shall be as
wool."   *Isaiah 1:18*

Blessed is he whose transgression is forgiven, whose
sin is covered. Blessed is the man to whom the LORD does
not impute iniquity, and in whose spirit there is no deceit.
                                                        Psalm 32:1–2

JESUS IS YOUR—Fellowship.

That which we have seen and heard we declare to you,
that you also may have fellowship with us; and truly our
fellowship is with the Father and with His Son Jesus
Christ.   *1 John 1:3*

God is faithful, by whom you were called into the fellowship of His Son, Jesus Christ our Lord.   *1 Corinthians 1:9*

"Behold, I stand at the door and knock. If anyone hears
My voice and opens the door, I will come in to him and
dine with him, and he with Me."   *Revelation 3:20*

"Sing and rejoice, O daughter of Zion! For behold, I am
coming and I will dwell in your midst," says the LORD.
                                                        Zechariah 2:10

Jesus answered and said to him, "If anyone loves Me, he will keep My word; and My Father will love him, and We will come to him and make Our home with him."

John 14:23

"For where two or three are gathered together in My name, I am there in the midst of them." *Matthew 18:20*

"Abide in Me, and I in you. As the branch cannot bear fruit of itself, unless it abides in the vine, neither can you, unless you abide in Me. I am the vine, you are the branches. He who abides in Me, and I in him, bears much fruit; for without Me you can do nothing.... If you abide in Me, and My words abide in you, you will ask what you desire, and it shall be done for you." *John 15:4–5, 7*

Therefore if there is any consolation in Christ, if any comfort of love, if any fellowship of the Spirit, if any affection and mercy, fulfill my joy by being like-minded, having the same love, being of one accord, of one mind.

Philippians 2:1–2

I am a companion of all who fear You, and of those who keep Your precepts. *Psalm 119:63*

And walk in love, as Christ also has loved us and given Himself for us, an offering and a sacrifice to God for a sweet-smelling aroma.... Speaking to one another in psalms and hymns and spiritual songs, singing and making melody in your heart to the Lord.... For we are members of His body, of His flesh and of His bones.

Ephesians 5:2, 19, 30

"He who has My commandments and keeps them, it is he who loves Me. And he who loves Me will be loved by My Father, and I will love him and manifest Myself to him."

John 14:21

This is the message which we have heard from Him and declare to you, that God is light and in Him is no darkness at all. If we say that we have fellowship with Him, and walk in darkness, we lie and do not practice the truth. But if we walk in the light as He is in the light, we have fellowship with one another, and the blood of Jesus Christ His Son cleanses us from all sin.

1 John 1:5–7

JESUS IS YOUR—Example.

For to this you were called, because Christ also suffered for us, leaving us an example, that you should follow His steps.

1 Peter 2:21

Therefore be imitators of God as dear children. And walk in love, as Christ also has loved us and given Himself for us, an offering and a sacrifice to God for a sweet-smelling aroma.

Ephesians 5:1–2

Let this mind be in you which was also in Christ Jesus, who, being in the form of God, did not consider it robbery to be equal with God, but made Himself of no reputation, taking the form of a bondservant, and coming in the likeness of men. And being found in appearance as a man, He humbled Himself and became obedient to the point of death, even the death of the cross.

Philippians 2:5–8

He who says he abides in Him ought himself also to walk just as He walked. *1 John 2:6*

"Yet it shall not be so among you; but whoever desires to become great among you shall be your servant. And whoever of you desires to be first shall be slave of all. For even the Son of Man did not come to be served, but to serve, and to give His life a ransom for many." *Mark 10:43–45*

"If I then, your Lord and Teacher, have washed your feet, you also ought to wash one another's feet. For I have given you an example, that you should do as I have done to you." *John 13:14, 15*

"A new commandment I give to you, that you love one another; as I have loved you, that you also love one another." *John 13:34*

By this we know love, because He laid down His life for us. And we also ought to lay down our lives for the brethren. *1 John 3:16*

Now may the God of patience and comfort grant you to be like-minded toward one another, according to Christ Jesus, that you may with one mind and one mouth glorify the God and Father of our Lord Jesus Christ. Therefore receive one another, just as Christ also received us, to the glory of God. *Romans 15:5–7*

Bearing with one another, and forgiving one another, if anyone has a complaint against another; even as Christ forgave you, so you also must do. *Colossians 3:13*

Looking unto Jesus, the author and finisher of our faith, who for the joy that was set before Him endured the cross, despising the shame, and has sat down at the right hand of the throne of God. For consider Him who endured such hostility from sinners against Himself, lest you become weary and discouraged in your souls.

Hebrews 12:2–3

JESUS IS YOUR—Security.

Blessed be the God and Father of our Lord Jesus Christ, who according to His abundant mercy has begotten us again to a living hope through the resurrection of Jesus Christ from the dead, to an inheritance incorruptible and undefiled and that does not fade away, reserved in heaven for you, who are kept by the power of God through faith for salvation ready to be revealed in the last time.

1 Peter 1:3–5

"My sheep hear My voice, and I know them, and they follow Me. And I give them eternal life, and they shall never perish; neither shall anyone snatch them out of My hand. My Father, who has given them to Me, is greater than all; and no one is able to snatch them out of My Father's hand."

John 10:27–29

For I am persuaded that neither death nor life, nor angels nor principalities nor powers, nor things present nor things to come, nor height nor depth, nor any other created thing, shall be able to separate us from the love of God which is in Christ Jesus our Lord. *Romans 8:38–39*

Being confident of this very thing, that He who has begun a good work in you will complete it until the day of Jesus Christ.   *Philippians 1:6*

But the Lord is faithful, who will establish you and guard you from the evil one.   *2 Thessalonians 3:3*

"All that the Father gives Me will come to Me, and the one who comes to Me I will by no means cast out."
                                                      John 6:37

Lift up your eyes on high, and see who has created these things, who brings out their host by number; he calls them all by name, by the greatness of His might and the strength of His power; not one is missing.   *Isaiah 40:26*

Surely goodness and mercy shall follow me all the days of my life; and I will dwell in the house of the LORD forever.
                                                      Psalm 23:6

"Do not labor for the food which perishes, but for the food which endures to everlasting life, which the Son of Man will give you, because God the Father has set His seal on Him."   *John 6:27*

Who also has sealed us and given us the Spirit in our hearts as a guarantee.   *2 Corinthians 1:22*

In Him you also trusted, after you heard the word of truth, the gospel of your salvation; in whom also, having believed, you were sealed with the Holy Spirit of promise.
                                                  Ephesians 1:13

Now to Him who is able to keep you from stumbling, and to present you faultless before the presence of His glory with exceeding joy, to God our Savior, who alone is wise, be glory and majesty, dominion and power, both now and forever. Amen.   *Jude 24–25*

And do not grieve the Holy Spirit of God, by whom you were sealed for the day of redemption.   *Ephesians 4:30*

And we desire that each one of you show the same diligence to the full assurance of hope until the end, that you do not become sluggish, but imitate those who through faith and patience inherit the promises.... That by two immutable things, in which it is impossible for God to lie, we might have strong consolation, who have fled for refuge to lay hold of the hope set before us. This hope we have as an anchor of the soul, both sure and steadfast, and which enters the Presence behind the veil, where the forerunner has entered for us, even Jesus, having become High Priest forever according to the order of Melchizedek.
Hebrews 6:11–12, 18–20

JESUS IS YOUR—Sufficiency.

And God is able to make all grace abound toward you, that you, always having all sufficiency in all things, may have an abundance for every good work.   *2 Corinthians 9:8*

"Therefore I say to you, whatever things you ask when you pray, believe that you receive them, and you will have them."   *Mark 11:24*

And my God shall supply all your need according to His riches in glory by Christ Jesus. *Philippians 4:19*

Not that we are sufficient of ourselves to think of anything as being from ourselves, but our sufficiency is from God. *2 Corinthians 3:5*

I can do all things through Christ who strengthens me. *Philippians 4:13*

And what is the exceeding greatness of His power toward us who believe, according to the working of His mighty power. *Ephesians 1:19*

And He said to me, "My grace is sufficient for you, for My strength is made perfect in weakness. Therefore most gladly I will rather boast in my infirmities, that the power of Christ may rest upon me." *2 Corinthians 12:9*

In all these things we are more than conquerors through Him who loved us. *Romans 8:37*

Blessed be the God and Father of our Lord Jesus Christ, who has blessed us with every spiritual blessing in the heavenly places in Christ. *Ephesians 1:3*

"If you abide in Me, and My words abide in you, you will ask what you desire, and it shall be done for you." *John 15:7*

"And whatever you ask in My name, that I will do, that the Father may be glorified in the Son." *John 14:13*

"And in that day you will ask Me nothing. Most assuredly, I say to you, whatever you ask the Father in My name He will give you. Until now you have asked nothing in My name. Ask, and you will receive, that your joy may be full."
John 16:23–24

"And whatever things you ask in prayer, believing, you will receive."
Matthew 21:22

He who did not spare His own Son, but delivered Him up for us all, how shall He not with Him also freely give us all things?
Romans 8:32

As His divine power has given to us all things that pertain to life and godliness, through the knowledge of Him who called us by glory and virtue, by which have been given to us exceedingly great and precious promises, that through these you may be partakers of the divine nature, having escaped the corruption that is in the world through lust.
2 Peter 1:3–4

Bless the Lord, O my soul, and forget not all His benefits: who forgives all your iniquities, who heals all your diseases, who redeems your life from destruction, who crowns you with lovingkindness and tender mercies.
Psalm 103:2–4

JESUS IS YOUR—Fulfillment.

"Blessed are those who hunger and thirst for righteousness, for they shall be filled."
Matthew 5:6

Delight yourself also in the LORD, and He shall give you the desires of your heart. *Psalm 37:4*

For He satisfies the longing soul, and fills the hungry soul with goodness. *Psalm 107:9*

Who satisfies your mouth with good things, so that your youth is renewed like the eagle's. *Psalm 103:5*

You shall eat in plenty and be satisfied, and praise the name of the LORD your God, who has dealt wondrously with you; and My people shall never be put to shame. *Joel 2:26*

And Jesus said to them, "I am the bread of life. He who comes to Me shall never hunger, and he who believes in Me shall never thirst." *John 6:35*

The poor shall eat and be satisfied; those who seek Him will praise the LORD. Let your heart live forever! *Psalm 22:26*

Jesus answered and said to her, "Whoever drinks of this water will thirst again, but whoever drinks of the water that I shall give him will never thirst. But the water that I shall give him will become in him a fountain of water springing up into everlasting life." *John 4:13, 14*

The LORD will answer and say to His people, "Behold, I will send you grain and new wine and oil, and you will be satisfied by them; I will no longer make you a reproach among the nations." *Joel 2:19*

If you extend your soul to the hungry and satisfy the afflicted soul, then your light shall dawn in the darkness, and your darkness shall be as the noonday. The LORD will guide you continually, and satisfy your soul in drought, and strengthen your bones; you shall be like a watered garden, and like a spring of water, whose waters do not fail.   *Isaiah 58:10–11*

The eyes of all look expectantly to You, and You give them their food in due season. You open Your hand and satisfy the desire of every living thing.   *Psalm 145:15–16*

Why do you spend money for what is not bread, and your wages for what does not satisfy? Listen carefully to Me, and eat what is good, and let your soul delight itself in abundance.   *Isaiah 55:2*

"I will satiate the soul of the priests with abundance, and My people shall be satisfied with My goodness, says the LORD."   *Jeremiah 31:14*

My soul shall be satisfied as with marrow and fatness, and my mouth shall praise You with joyful lips. When I remember You on my bed, I meditate on You in the night watches.   *Psalm 63:5–6*

He who did not spare His own Son, but delivered Him up for us all, how shall He not with Him also freely give us all things?   *Romans 8:32*

JESUS IS YOUR—Everything.

And my God shall supply all your need according to His riches in glory by Christ Jesus.   *Philippians 4:19*

I can do all things through Christ who strengthens me.
Philippians 4:13

Yet in all these things we are more than conquerors through Him who loved us.   *Romans 8:37*

Therefore let no one boast in men. For all things are yours: whether Paul or Apollos or Cephas, or the world or life or death, or things present or things to come—all are yours. And you are Christ's, and Christ is God's.
1 Corinthians 3:21–23

"If you abide in Me, and My words abide in you, you will ask what you desire, and it shall be done for you."   *John 15:7*

"And in that day you will ask Me nothing. Most assuredly, I say to you, whatever you ask the Father in My name He will give you. Until now you have asked nothing in My name. Ask, and you will receive, that your joy may be full."
John 16:23–24

"And whatever things you ask in prayer, believing, you will receive."   *Matthew 21:22*

"Therefore I say to you, whatever things you ask when you pray, believe that you receive them, and you will have them."
Mark 11:24

Blessed be the God and Father of our Lord Jesus Christ, who has blessed us with every spiritual blessing in the heavenly places in Christ.   *Ephesians 1:3*

And whatever we ask we receive from Him, because we keep His commandments and do those things that are pleasing in His sight.   *1 John 3:22*

For He made Him who knew no sin to be sin for us, that we might become the righteousness of God in Him.
                    2 Corinthians 5:21

For to me, to live is Christ, and to die is gain.
                    Philippians 1:21

Therefore, if anyone is in Christ, he is a new creation; old things have passed away; behold, all things have become new.   *2 Corinthians 5:17*

Now to Him who is able to do exceedingly abundantly above all that we ask or think, according to the power that works in us, to Him be glory in the church by Christ Jesus to all generations, forever and ever. Amen.
                    Ephesians 3:20–21

And God is able to make all grace abound toward you, that you, always having all sufficiency in all things, may have an abundance for every good work.   *2 Corinthians 9:8*

Blessed be the Lord, who daily loads us with benefits, the God of our salvation!   *Psalm 68:19*

THE BIBLE IS YOUR—Infallible Authority.

All Scripture is given by inspiration of God, and is profitable for doctrine, for reproof, for correction, for instruction in righteousness. *2 Timothy 3:16*

Knowing this first, that no prophecy of Scripture is of any private interpretation, for prophecy never came by the will of man, but holy men of God spoke as they were moved by the Holy Spirit. *2 Peter 1:20–21*

For the word of God is living and powerful, and sharper than any two-edged sword, piercing even to the division of soul and spirit, and of joints and marrow, and is a discerner of the thoughts and intents of the heart. *Hebrews 4:12*

"For as the rain comes down, and the snow from heaven, and do not return there, but water the earth, and make it bring forth and bud, that it may give seed to the sower and bread to the eater, so shall My word be that goes forth from My mouth; it shall not return to Me void, but it shall accomplish what I please, and it shall prosper in the thing for which I sent it." *Isaiah 55:10–11*

"You search the Scriptures, for in them you think you have eternal life; and these are they which testify of Me." *John 5:39*

Having been born again, not of corruptible seed but incorruptible, through the word of God which lives and abides forever. *1 Peter 1:23*

For He spoke, and it was done; he commanded, and it stood fast. *Psalm 33:9*

Every word of God is pure. *Proverbs 30:5*

Forever, O LORD, your word is settled in heaven.
Psalm 119:89

By the word of the LORD the heavens were made, and all the host of them by the breath of His mouth. *Psalm 33:6*

For all the promises of God in Him are Yes, and in Him Amen, to the glory of God through us. *2 Corinthians 1:20*

Because "All flesh is as grass, and all the glory of man as the flower of the grass. The grass withers, and its flower falls away, but the word of the LORD endures forever."
1 Peter 1:24–25

"Heaven and earth will pass away, but My words will by no means pass away." *Mark 13:31*

THE BIBLE IS YOUR—Guide for Life.

Your word is a lamp to my feet, and a light to my path.
Psalm 119:105

When you roam, they will lead you; when you sleep, they will keep you; and when you awake, they will speak with you. For the commandment is a lamp, and the law a light. *Proverbs 6:22–23*

Your word I have hidden in my heart, that I might not sin against You. *Psalm 119:11*

Moreover by them Your servant is warned, and in keeping them there is great reward. *Psalm 19:11*

How can a young man cleanse his way? By taking heed according to Your word. *Psalm 119:9*

Then Jesus said to those Jews who believed Him, "If you abide in My word, you are My disciples indeed. And you shall know the truth, and the truth shall make you free." *John 8:31–32*

Your testimonies also are my delight and my counselors. *Psalm 119:24*

By which have been given to us exceedingly great and precious promises, that through these you may be partakers of the divine nature, having escaped the corruption that is in the world through lust. *2 Peter 1:4*

The steps of a good man are ordered by the Lord, and He delights in his way. *Psalm 37:23*

I will instruct you and teach you in the way you should go; I will guide you with My eye. *Psalm 32:8*

He restores my soul; he leads me in the paths of righteousness for His name's sake. *Psalm 23:3*

Your ears shall hear a word behind you, saying, "This is the way, walk in it," whenever you turn to the right hand or whenever you turn to the left.   *Isaiah 30:21*

As He spoke by the mouth of His holy prophets, who have been since the world began.... To give light to those who sit in darkness and the shadow of death, to guide our feet into the way of peace.   *Luke 1:70, 79*

This Book of the Law shall not depart from your mouth, but you shall meditate in it day and night, that you may observe to do according to all that is written in it. For then you will make your way prosperous, and then you will have good success.   *Joshua 1:8*

All Scripture is given by inspiration of God, and is profitable for doctrine, for reproof, for correction, for instruction in righteousness, that the man of God may be complete, thoroughly equipped for every good work.
                    2 Timothy 3:16–17

THE BIBLE IS YOUR—Strength.

And he said, "O man greatly beloved, fear not! Peace be to you; be strong, yes, be strong!" So when he spoke to me I was strengthened, and said, "Let my lord speak, for you have strengthened me."   *Daniel 10:19*

My soul melts from heaviness; strengthen me according to Your word.   *Psalm 119:28*

For thus says the Lord God, the Holy One of Israel: "In returning and rest you shall be saved; in quietness and confidence shall be your strength." But you would not.

Isaiah 30:15

That He would grant you, according to the riches of His glory, to be strengthened with might through His Spirit in the inner man, that Christ may dwell in your hearts through faith.

Ephesians 3:16–17

That you may walk worthy of the Lord, fully pleasing Him, being fruitful in every good work and increasing in the knowledge of God; strengthened with all might, according to His glorious power, for all patience and long-suffering with joy; giving thanks to the Father who has qualified us to be partakers of the inheritance of the saints in the light.

Colossians 1:10–12

But those who wait on the Lord shall renew their strength; they shall mount up with wings like eagles, they shall run and not be weary, they shall walk and not faint.

Isaiah 40:31

Then he said to them, "Go your way, eat the fat, drink the sweet, and send portions to those for whom nothing is prepared; for this day is holy to our Lord. Do not sorrow, for the joy of the Lord is your strength."

Nehemiah 8:10

I can do all things through Christ who strengthens me.

Philippians 4:13

Fear not, for I am with you; be not dismayed, for I am your God. I will strengthen you, yes, I will help you, I will uphold you with My righteous right hand.   *Isaiah 41:10*

Counsel is mine, and sound wisdom; I am understanding, I have strength.   *Proverbs 8:14*

He gives power to the weak, and to those who have no might He increases strength.   *Isaiah 40:29*

The Lord is my rock and my fortress and my deliverer; my God, my strength, in whom I will trust.   *Psalm 18:2*

Therefore take up the whole armor of God, that you may be able to withstand in the evil day, and having done all, to stand.   *Ephesians 6:13*

The Lord is my light and my salvation; whom shall I fear? The Lord is the strength of my life; of whom shall I be afraid?   *Psalm 27:1*

Finally, my brethren, be strong in the Lord and in the power of His might.   *Ephesians 6:10*

WHAT TO DO WHEN YOU FEEL—Discouraged.

So the ransomed of the Lord shall return, and come to Zion with singing, with everlasting joy on their heads. They shall obtain joy and gladness; sorrow and sighing shall flee away.   *Isaiah 51:11*

In this you greatly rejoice, though now for a little while, if need be, you have been grieved by various trials, that the genuineness of your faith, being much more precious than gold that perishes, though it is tested by fire, may be found to praise, honor, and glory at the revelation of Jesus Christ, whom having not seen you love. Though now you do not see Him, yet believing, you rejoice with joy inexpressible and full of glory, receiving the end of your faith—the salvation of your souls. *1 Peter 1:6–9*

Be anxious for nothing, but in everything by prayer and supplication, with thanksgiving, let your requests be made known to God; and the peace of God, which surpasses all understanding, will guard your hearts and minds through Christ Jesus. Finally, brethren, whatever things are true, whatever things are noble, whatever things are just, whatever things are pure, whatever things are lovely, whatever things are of good report, if there is any virtue and if there is anything praiseworthy—meditate on these things. *Philippians 4:6–8*

Though I walk in the midst of trouble, You will revive me; you will stretch out Your hand against the wrath of my enemies, and Your right hand will save me. *Psalm 138:7*

"Let not your heart be troubled; you believe in God, believe also in Me." *John 14:1*

"Peace I leave with you, My peace I give to you; not as the world gives do I give to you. Let not your heart be troubled, neither let it be afraid." *John 14:27*

The LORD is my light and my salvation; whom shall I fear? The LORD is the strength of my life; of whom shall I be afraid? When the wicked came against me to eat up my flesh, my enemies and foes, they stumbled and fell. Though an army may encamp against me, my heart shall not fear; though war may rise against me, in this I will be confident. One thing I have desired of the LORD, that will I seek: that I may dwell in the house of the LORD all the days of my life, to behold the beauty of the LORD, and to inquire in His temple. For in the time of trouble he shall hide me in His pavilion; in the secret place of His tabernacle He shall hide me; He shall set me high upon a rock. And now my head shall be lifted up above my enemies all around me; therefore I will offer sacrifices of joy in His tabernacle; I will sing, yes, I will sing praises to the LORD. Hear, O LORD, when I cry with my voice! Have mercy also upon me, and answer me. When You said, "Seek My face," my heart said to You, "Your face, LORD, I will seek." Do not hide Your face from me; do not turn Your servant away in anger; you have been my help; do not leave me nor forsake me, O God of my salvation. When my father and my mother forsake me, then the LORD will take care of me. Teach me Your way, O LORD, and lead me in a smooth path, because of my enemies. Do not deliver me to the will of my adversaries; for false witnesses have risen against me, and such as breathe out violence. I would have lost heart, unless I had believed that I would see the goodness of the LORD in the land of the living. Wait on the LORD; be of good courage, and He shall strengthen your heart; wait, I say, on the LORD!

Psalm 27:1–14

We are hard-pressed on every side, yet not crushed;
we are perplexed, but not in despair; persecuted, but not
forsaken; struck down, but not destroyed.

2 Corinthians 4:8–9

Therefore do not cast away your confidence, which
has great reward. For you have need of endurance, so that
after you have done the will of God, you may receive the
promise. *Hebrews 10:35–36*

Being confident of this very thing, that He who has
begun a good work in you will complete it until the day of
Jesus Christ. *Philippians 1:6*

And let us not grow weary while doing good, for in due
season we shall reap if we do not lose heart. *Galatians 6:9*

Be of good courage, and He shall strengthen your
heart, all you who hope in the LORD. *Psalm 31:24*

WHAT TO DO WHEN YOU FEEL—Worried.

Casting all your care upon Him, for He cares for you.

1 Peter 5:7

Be anxious for nothing, but in everything by prayer
and supplication, with thanksgiving, let your requests
be made known to God; and the peace of God, which
surpasses all understanding, will guard your hearts and
minds through Christ Jesus. *Philippians 4:6–7*

"Let not your heart be troubled; you believe in God, believe also in Me."   *John 14:1*

I will both lie down in peace, and sleep; for You alone, O LORD, make me dwell in safety.   *Psalm 4:8*

And my God shall supply all your need according to His riches in glory by Christ Jesus.   *Philippians 4:19*

"Therefore I say to you, do not worry about your life, what you will eat or what you will drink; nor about your body, what you will put on. Is not life more than food and the body more than clothing? Look at the birds of the air, for they neither sow nor reap nor gather into barns; yet your heavenly Father feeds them. Are you not of more value than they? Which of you by worrying can add one cubit to his stature? So why do you worry about clothing? Consider the lilies of the field, how they grow: they neither toil nor spin; and yet I say to you that even Solomon in all his glory was not arrayed like one of these. Now if God so clothes the grass of the field, which today is, and tomorrow is thrown into the oven, will He not much more clothe you, O you of little faith? Therefore do not worry, saying, 'What shall we eat?' or 'What shall we drink?' or 'What shall we wear?' For after all these things the Gentiles seek. For your heavenly Father knows that you need all these things. But seek first the kingdom of God and His righteousness, and all these things shall be added to you. Therefore do not worry about tomorrow, for tomorrow will worry about its own things. Sufficient for the day is its own trouble."   *Matthew 6:25–34*

And let the peace of God rule in your hearts, to which also you were called in one body; and be thankful.
Colossians 3:15

You will keep him in perfect peace, whose mind is stayed on You, because he trusts in You. *Isaiah 26:3*

For to be carnally minded is death, but to be spiritually minded is life and peace. *Romans 8:6*

When you lie down, you will not be afraid; yes, you will lie down and your sleep will be sweet. *Proverbs 3:24*

For we who have believed do enter that rest, as He has said: "So I swore in My wrath, 'They shall not enter My rest,'" although the works were finished from the foundation of the world.... There remains therefore a rest for the people of God. *Hebrews 4:3, 9*

Great peace have those who love Your law, and nothing causes them to stumble. *Psalm 119:165*

He who dwells in the secret place of the Most High shall abide under the shadow of the Almighty. I will say of the LORD, "He is my refuge and my fortress; my God, in Him I will trust." *Psalm 91:1–2*

"Peace I leave with you, My peace I give to you; not as the world gives do I give to you. Let not your heart be troubled, neither let it be afraid." *John 14:27*

WHAT TO DO WHEN YOU FEEL—Lonely.

Let your conduct be without covetousness; be content with such things as you have. For He Himself has said, "I will never leave you nor forsake you."   *Hebrews 13:5*

"Teaching them to observe all things that I have commanded you; and lo, I am with you always, even to the end of the age." Amen.   *Matthew 28:20*

For the LORD will not forsake His people, for His great name's sake, because it has pleased the LORD to make you His people.   *1 Samuel 12:22*

Fear not, for I am with you; be not dismayed, for I am your God. I will strengthen you, yes, I will help you, I will uphold you with My righteous right hand.   *Isaiah 41:10*

"I will not leave you orphans; I will come to you."
          John 14:18

"Let not your heart be troubled; you believe in God, believe also in Me."   *John 14:1*

The eternal God is your refuge, and underneath are the everlasting arms; He will thrust out the enemy from before you, and will say, "Destroy!"   *Deuteronomy 33:27*

He heals the brokenhearted and binds up their wounds.   *Psalm 147:3*

Who shall separate us from the love of Christ? Shall tribulation, or distress, or persecution, or famine, or nakedness, or peril, or sword? As it is written: "For Your sake we are killed all day long; we are accounted as sheep for the slaughter." Yet in all these things we are more than conquerors through Him who loved us. For I am persuaded that neither death nor life, nor angels nor principalities nor powers, nor things present nor things to come, nor height nor depth, nor any other created thing, shall be able to separate us from the love of God which is in Christ Jesus our Lord.   *Romans 8:35–39*

(For the Lord your God is a merciful God), He will not forsake you nor destroy you, nor forget the covenant of your fathers which He swore to them.   *Deuteronomy 4:31*

"Be strong and of good courage, do not fear nor be afraid of them; for the Lord your God, He is the One who goes with you. He will not leave you nor forsake you."
Deuteronomy 31:6

When my father and my mother forsake me, then the Lord will take care of me.   *Psalm 27:10*

"For the mountains shall depart and the hills be removed, but My kindness shall not depart from you, nor shall My covenant of peace be removed," says the Lord, who has mercy on you.   *Isaiah 54:10*

Casting all your care upon Him, for He cares for you.
1 Peter 5:7

God is our refuge and strength, a very present help in trouble. *Psalm 46:1*

WHAT TO DO WHEN YOU FEEL—Tempted.

Therefore let him who thinks he stands take heed lest he fall. No temptation has overtaken you except such as is common to man; but God is faithful, who will not allow you to be tempted beyond what you are able, but with the temptation will also make the way of escape, that you may be able to bear it. *1 Corinthians 10:12–13*

Seeing then that we have a great High Priest who has passed through the heavens, Jesus the Son of God, let us hold fast our confession. For we do not have a High Priest who cannot sympathize with our weaknesses, but was in all points tempted as we are, yet without sin. Let us therefore come boldly to the throne of grace, that we may obtain mercy and find grace to help in time of need. *Hebrews 4:14–16*

For in that He Himself has suffered, being tempted, He is able to aid those who are tempted. *Hebrews 2:18*

Then the Lord knows how to deliver the godly out of temptations and to reserve the unjust under punishment for the day of judgment. *2 Peter 2:9*

For sin shall not have dominion over you, for you are not under law but under grace. *Romans 6:14*

Your word I have hidden in my heart, that I might not sin against You.

Psalm 119:11

Let no one say when he is tempted, "I am tempted by God"; for God cannot be tempted by evil, nor does He Himself tempt anyone. But each one is tempted when he is drawn away by his own desires and enticed.

James 1:13–14

He who covers his sins will not prosper, but whoever confesses and forsakes them will have mercy.

Proverbs 28:13

If we confess our sins, He is faithful and just to forgive us our sins and to cleanse us from all unrighteousness.

1 John 1:9

Be sober, be vigilant; because your adversary the devil walks about like a roaring lion, seeking whom he may devour. Resist him, steadfast in the faith, knowing that the same sufferings are experienced by your brotherhood in the world.

1 Peter 5:8–9

Finally, my brethren, be strong in the Lord and in the power of His might. Put on the whole armor of God, that you may be able to stand against the wiles of the devil. . . . Above all, taking the shield of faith with which you will be able to quench all the fiery darts of the wicked one.

Ephesians 6:10–11, 16

Therefore submit to God. Resist the devil and he will flee from you.

James 4:7

You are of God, little children, and have overcome them, because He who is in you is greater than he who is in the world.   *1 John 4:4*

My brethren, count it all joy when you fall into various trials, knowing that the testing of your faith produces patience.... Blessed is the man who endures temptation; for when he has been approved, he will receive the crown of life which the Lord has promised to those who love Him.
                                                    James 1:2–3, 12

Now to Him who is able to keep you from stumbling, and to present you faultless before the presence of His glory with exceeding joy, to God our Savior, who alone is wise, be glory and majesty, dominion and power, both now and forever. Amen.   *Jude 24–25*

In this you greatly rejoice, though now for a little while, if need be, you have been grieved by various trials, that the genuineness of your faith, being much more precious than gold that perishes, though it is tested by fire, may be found to praise, honor, and glory at the revelation of Jesus Christ.
                                                      1 Peter 1:6–7

WHAT TO DO WHEN YOU FEEL—Rebellious.

Obey those who rule over you, and be submissive, for they watch out for your souls, as those who must give account. Let them do so with joy and not with grief, for that would be unprofitable for you.   *Hebrews 13:17*

A wise man fears and departs from evil, but a fool rages and is self confident. A quick-tempered man acts foolishly, and a man of wicked intentions is hated.

Proverbs 14:16–17

So Samuel said: "Has the LORD as great delight in burnt offerings and sacrifices, as in obeying the voice of the LORD? Behold, to obey is better than sacrifice, and to heed than the fat of rams. For rebellion is as the sin of witchcraft, and stubbornness is as iniquity and idolatry. Because you have rejected the word of the LORD, He also has rejected you from being king." *1 Samuel 15:22–23*

Therefore gird up the loins of your mind, be sober, and rest your hope fully upon the grace that is to be brought to you at the revelation of Jesus Christ; as obedient children, not conforming yourselves to the former lusts, as in your ignorance. *1 Peter 1:13–14*

"If you are willing and obedient, you shall eat the good of the land; but if you refuse and rebel, you shall be devoured by the sword"; for the mouth of the LORD has spoken. *Isaiah 1:19–20*

Therefore submit yourselves to every ordinance of man for the Lord's sake, whether to the king as supreme, or to governors, as to those who are sent by him for the punishment of evildoers and for the praise of those who do good. For this is the will of God, that by doing good you may put to silence the ignorance of foolish men. *1 Peter 2:13–15*

Let this mind be in you which was also in Christ Jesus, who, being in the form of God, did not consider it robbery to be equal with God, but made Himself of no reputation, taking the form of a bondservant, and coming in the likeness of men. And being found in appearance as a man, He humbled Himself and became obedient to the point of death, even the death of the cross.   *Philippians 2:5–8*

Though He was a Son, yet He learned obedience by the things which He suffered.   *Hebrews 5:8*

Likewise you younger people, submit yourselves to your elders. Yes, all of you be submissive to one another, and be clothed with humility, for "God resists the proud, but gives grace to the humble." Therefore humble yourselves under the mighty hand of God, that He may exalt you in due time.   *1 Peter 5:5–6*

Submitting to one another in the fear of God.
    Ephesians 5:21

No grave trouble will overtake the righteous, but the wicked shall be filled with evil.   *Proverbs 12:21*

Therefore do not let sin reign in your mortal body, that you should obey it in its lusts. And do not present your members as instruments of unrighteousness to sin, but present yourselves to God as being alive from the dead, and your members as instruments of righteousness to God.   *Romans 6:12–13*

This I say, therefore, and testify in the Lord, that you should no longer walk as the rest of the Gentiles walk, in the futility of their mind, having their understanding darkened, being alienated from the life of God, because of the ignorance that is in them, because of the blindness of their heart.   *Ephesians 4:17–18*

For you were once darkness, but now you are light in the Lord. Walk as children of light.   *Ephesians 5:8*

Therefore submit to God. Resist the devil and he will flee from you.   *James 4:7*

WHAT TO DO WHEN YOU ARE—in Need of Peace.

You will keep him in perfect peace, whose mind is stayed on You, because he trusts in You.   *Isaiah 26:3*

"Peace I leave with you, My peace I give to you; not as the world gives do I give to you. Let not your heart be troubled, neither let it be afraid."   *John 14:27*

Be anxious for nothing, but in everything by prayer and supplication, with thanksgiving, let your requests be made known to God; and the peace of God, which surpasses all understanding, will guard your hearts and minds through Christ Jesus.   *Philippians 4:6–7*

Therefore, having been justified by faith, we have peace with God through our Lord Jesus Christ.   *Romans 5:1*

LORD, You will establish peace for us, for You have also done all our works in us. *Isaiah 26:12*

For you shall go out with joy, and be led out with peace; the mountains and the hills shall break forth into singing before you, and all the trees of the field shall clap their hands. *Isaiah 55:12*

Mark the blameless man, and observe the upright; for the future of that man is peace. *Psalm 37:37*

For to be carnally minded is death, but to be spiritually minded is life and peace. *Romans 8:6*

Great peace have those who love Your law, and nothing causes them to stumble. *Psalm 119:165*

He shall enter into peace; they shall rest in their beds, each one walking in his uprightness. *Isaiah 57:2*

For the kingdom of God is not eating and drinking, but righteousness and peace and joy in the Holy Spirit. For he who serves Christ in these things is acceptable to God and approved by men. Therefore let us pursue the things which make for peace and the things by which one may edify another. *Romans 14:17–19*

Finally, brethren, farewell. Become complete. Be of good comfort, be of one mind, live in peace; and the God of love and peace will be with you. *2 Corinthians 13:11*

But the meek shall inherit the earth, and shall delight themselves in the abundance of peace. *Psalm 37:11*

Now may the God of hope fill you with all joy and peace in believing, that you may abound in hope by the power of the Holy Spirit. *Romans 15:13*

WHAT TO DO WHEN YOU ARE—Lukewarm Spiritually.

"Be watchful, and strengthen the things which remain, that are ready to die, for I have not found your works perfect before God.... I know your works, that you are neither cold nor hot. I could wish you were cold or hot. So then, because you are lukewarm, and neither cold nor hot, I will vomit you out of My mouth." *Revelation 3:2, 15–16*

"Nevertheless I have this against you, that you have left your first love." *Revelation 2:4*

O Ephraim, what shall I do to you? O Judah, what shall I do to you? For your faithfulness is like a morning cloud, and like the early dew it goes away. *Hosea 6:4*

Only take heed to yourself, and diligently keep yourself, lest you forget the things your eyes have seen, and lest they depart from your heart all the days of your life. And teach them to your children and your grandchildren.

Deuteronomy 4:9

Beware that you do not forget the LORD your God by not keeping His commandments, His judgments, and His statutes which I command you today, lest—when you have eaten and are full, and have built beautiful houses and dwell in them; and when your herds and your flocks multiply, and your silver and your gold are multiplied, and all that you have is multiplied; when your heart is lifted up, and you forget the LORD your God who brought you out of the land of Egypt, from the house of bondage.

Deuteronomy 8:11–14

If we had forgotten the name of our God, or stretched out our hands to a foreign god, would not God search this out? For He knows the secrets of the heart.

Psalm 44:20–21

Beware, brethren, lest there be in any of you an evil heart of unbelief in departing from the living God; but exhort one another daily, while it is called "Today," lest any of you be hardened through the deceitfulness of sin.

Hebrews 3:12–13

Of whom we have much to say, and hard to explain, since you have become dull of hearing. For though by this time you ought to be teachers, you need someone to teach you again the first principles of the oracles of God; and you have come to need milk and not solid food.

Hebrews 5:11–12

Looking carefully lest anyone fall short of the grace of God; lest any root of bitterness springing up cause trouble, and by this many become defiled. *Hebrews 12:15*

For if, after they have escaped the pollutions of the world through the knowledge of the Lord and Savior Jesus Christ, they are again entangled in them and overcome, the latter end is worse for them than the beginning. For it would have been better for them not to have known the way of righteousness, than having known it, to turn from the holy commandment delivered to them.   *2 Peter 2:20–21*

Thus says the Lord: "Stand in the ways and see, and ask for the old paths, where the good way is, and walk in it; then you will find rest for your souls. But they said, 'We will not walk in it.'"   *Jeremiah 6:16*

If we confess our sins, He is faithful and just to forgive us our sins and to cleanse us from all unrighteousness.   *1 John 1:9*

"Yet from the days of your fathers you have gone away from My ordinances and have not kept them. Return to Me, and I will return to you," says the Lord of hosts. "But you said, 'In what way shall we return?'"   *Malachi 3:7*

WHAT TO DO WHEN YOU ARE—in Grief.

But I do not want you to be ignorant, brethren, concerning those who have fallen asleep, lest you sorrow as others who have no hope. For if we believe that Jesus died and rose again, even so God will bring with Him those who sleep in Jesus.   *1 Thessalonians 4:13–14*

For the Lord has comforted His people, and will have mercy on His afflicted.   *Isaiah 49:13*

74

When you pass through the waters, I will be with you; and through the rivers, they shall not overflow you. When you walk through the fire, you shall not be burned, nor shall the flame scorch you. *Isaiah 43:2*

Now may our Lord Jesus Christ Himself, and our God and Father, who has loved us and given us everlasting consolation and good hope by grace, comfort your hearts and establish you in every good word and work.
2 Thessalonians 2:16–17

"Blessed are those who mourn, for they shall be comforted." *Matthew 5:4*

Blessed be the God and Father of our Lord Jesus Christ, the Father of mercies and God of all comfort, who comforts us in all our tribulation, that we may be able to comfort those who are in any trouble, with the comfort with which we ourselves are comforted by God.
2 Corinthians 1:3–4

"The Spirit of the Lord God is upon Me, because the Lord has anointed Me to preach good tidings to the poor; He has sent Me to heal the brokenhearted, to proclaim liberty to the captives, and the opening of the prison to those who are bound; to proclaim the acceptable year of the Lord, and the day of vengeance of our God; to comfort all who mourn, to console those who mourn in Zion, to give them beauty for ashes, the oil of joy for mourning, the garment of praise for the spirit of heaviness; that they may be called trees of righteousness, the planting of the Lord, that He may be glorified." *Isaiah 61:1–3*

This is my comfort in my affliction, for Your word has given me life.   *Psalm 119:50*

"O Death, where is your sting? O Hades, where is your victory?" The sting of death is sin, and the strength of sin is the law. But thanks be to God, who gives us the victory through our Lord Jesus Christ.   *1 Corinthians 15:55–57*

Yea, though I walk through the valley of the shadow of death, I will fear no evil; for You are with me; Your rod and Your staff, they comfort me.   *Psalm 23:4*

For we do not have a High Priest who cannot sympathize with our weaknesses, but was in all points tempted as we are, yet without sin. Let us therefore come boldly to the throne of grace, that we may obtain mercy and find grace to help in time of need.   *Hebrews 4:15–16*

Fear not, for I am with you; be not dismayed, for I am your God. I will strengthen you, yes, I will help you, I will uphold you with My righteous right hand.   *Isaiah 41:10*

So the ransomed of the LORD shall return, and come to Zion with singing, with everlasting joy on their heads. They shall obtain joy and gladness; sorrow and sighing shall flee away.   *Isaiah 51:11*

We are confident, yes, well pleased rather to be absent from the body and to be present with the Lord.
                                                    2 Corinthians 5:8

Casting all your care upon Him, for He cares for you.

1 Peter 5:7

"And God will wipe away every tear from their eyes; there shall be no more death, nor sorrow, nor crying. There shall be no more pain, for the former things have passed away."

Revelation 21:4

WHAT TO DO WHEN YOU ARE—in Doubt About God.

So Jesus answered and said to them, "Have faith in God. For assuredly, I say to you, whoever says to this mountain, 'Be removed and be cast into the sea,' and does not doubt in his heart, but believes that those things he says will be done, he will have whatever he says. Therefore I say to you, whatever things you ask when you pray, believe that you receive them, and you will have them."

Mark 11:22–24

"And do not seek what you should eat or what you should drink, nor have an anxious mind. For all these things the nations of the world seek after, and your Father knows that you need these things. But seek the kingdom of God, and all these things shall be added to you."

Luke 12:29–31

He did not waver at the promise of God through unbelief, but was strengthened in faith, giving glory to God, And being fully convinced that what He had promised He was also able to perform.

Romans 4:20–21

"My counsel shall stand, and I will do all My pleasure . . ." Indeed I have spoken it; I will also bring it to pass. I have purposed it; I will also do it."   *Isaiah 46:10–11*

He who calls you is faithful, who also will do it.
1 Thessalonians 5:24

The Lord is not slack concerning His promise, as some count slackness, but is longsuffering toward us, not willing that any should perish but that all should come to repentance.   *2 Peter 3:9*

As for God, His way is perfect; the word of the Lord is proven; He is a shield to all who trust in Him.   *Psalm 18:30*

Behold, the Lord's hand is not shortened, that it cannot save; nor His ear heavy, that it cannot hear.   *Isaiah 59:1*

Beloved, do not think it strange concerning the fiery trial which is to try you, as though some strange thing happened to you; but rejoice to the extent that you partake of Christ's sufferings, that when His glory is revealed, you may also be glad with exceeding joy.   *1 Peter 4:12–13*

For as the rain comes down, and the snow from heaven, and do not return there, but water the earth, and make it bring forth and bud, that it may give seed to the sower and bread to the eater, so shall My word be that goes forth from My mouth; it shall not return to Me void, but it shall accomplish what I please, and it shall prosper in the thing for which I sent it.   *Isaiah 55:10–11*

So then faith comes by hearing, and hearing by the word of God.   *Romans 10:17*

WHAT TO DO WHEN—Troubles Hit Your Life.

The Lord is good, a stronghold in the day of trouble; and He knows those who trust in Him.   *Nahum 1:7*

We are hard pressed on every side, yet not crushed; we are perplexed, but not in despair; persecuted, but not forsaken; struck down, but not destroyed.
2 Corinthians 4:8–9

Though I walk in the midst of trouble, You will revive me; You will stretch out Your hand against the wrath of my enemies, and Your right hand will save me.   *Psalm 138:7*

"Let not your heart be troubled; you believe in God, believe also in Me."   *John 14:1*

When you pass through the waters, I will be with you; and through the rivers, they shall not overflow you. When you walk through the fire, you shall not be burned, nor shall the flame scorch you.   *Isaiah 43:2*

And we know that all things work together for good to those who love God, to those who are the called according to His purpose.   *Romans 8:28*

I will be glad and rejoice in Your mercy, for You have considered my trouble.   *Psalm 31:7*

I will lift up my eyes to the hills— from whence comes my help? My help comes from the Lord, who made heaven and earth.   *Psalm 121:1–2*

For we do not have a High Priest who cannot sympathize with our weaknesses, but was in all points tempted as we are, yet without sin. Let us therefore come boldly to the throne of grace, that we may obtain mercy and find grace to help in time of need.   *Hebrews 4:15–16*

"Therefore do not worry about tomorrow, for tomorrow will worry about its own things. Sufficient for the day is its own trouble."   *Matthew 6:34*

Blessed be the God and Father of our Lord Jesus Christ, the Father of mercies and God of all comfort, who comforts us in all our tribulation, that we may be able to comfort those who are in any trouble, with the comfort with which we ourselves are comforted by God.
                                                        2 Corinthians 1:3–4

Be anxious for nothing, but in everything by prayer and supplication, with thanksgiving, let your requests be made known to God; and the peace of God, which surpasses all understanding, will guard your hearts and minds through Christ Jesus.   *Philippians 4:6–7*

So the ransomed of the Lord shall return, and come to Zion with singing, with everlasting joy on their heads. They shall obtain joy and gladness; sorrow and sighing shall flee away.   *Isaiah 51:11*

WHAT TO DO WHEN—You Have Physical Sickness.

Beloved, I pray that you may prosper in all things and be in health, just as your soul prospers.   *3 John 2*

Then Jesus went about all the cities and villages, teaching in their synagogues, preaching the gospel of the kingdom, and healing every sickness and every disease among the people.   *Matthew 9:35*

And the whole multitude sought to touch Him, for power went out from Him and healed them all.   *Luke 6:19*

Jesus Christ is the same yesterday, today, and forever.   *Hebrews 13:8*

Himself bore our sins in His own body on the tree, that we, having died to sins, might live for righteousness—by whose stripes you were healed.   *1 Peter 2:24*

Who forgives all your iniquities, who heals all your diseases.   *Psalm 103:3*

But He was wounded for our transgressions, He was bruised for our iniquities; the chastisement for our peace was upon Him, and by His stripes we are healed.   *Isaiah 53:5*

Heal me, O Lord, and I shall be healed; save me, and I shall be saved, for You are my praise.   *Jeremiah 17:14*

"For I will restore health to you and heal you of your wounds," says the Lord.   *Jeremiah 30:17*

If you diligently heed the voice of the L ORD your God and do what is right in His sight, give ear to His commandments and keep all His statutes, I will put none of the diseases on you which I have brought on the Egyptians. For I am the L ORD who heals you.　　*Exodus 15:26*

My son, give attention to my words; incline your ear to my sayings. Do not let them depart from your eyes; keep them in the midst of your heart; for they are life to those who find them, and health to all their flesh.

Proverbs 4:20–22

He sent His word and healed them, and delivered them from their destructions.　　*Psalm 107:20*

The centurion answered and said, "Lord, I am not worthy that You should come under my roof. But only speak a word, and my servant will be healed."　　*Matthew 8:8*

Is anyone among you sick? Let him call for the elders of the church, and let them pray over him, anointing him with oil in the name of the Lord. And the prayer of faith will save the sick, and the Lord will raise him up. And if he has committed sins, he will be forgiven.　　*James 5:14–15*

"And these signs will follow those who believe: In My name they will cast out demons; they will speak with new tongues; they will take up serpents; and if they drink anything deadly, it will by no means hurt them; they will lay hands on the sick, and they will recover."

Mark 16:17–18

WHAT TO DO WHEN YOU ARE—in Financial Trouble.

Beloved, I pray that you may prosper in all things and be in health, just as your soul prospers. *3 John 2*

I have been young, and now am old; yet I have not seen the righteous forsaken, nor his descendants begging bread. *Psalm 37:25*

The young lions lack and suffer hunger; but those who seek the LORD shall not lack any good thing. *Psalm 34:10*

The LORD is my shepherd; I shall not want. *Psalm 23:1*

And all these blessings shall come upon you and overtake you, because you obey the voice of the LORD your God: "Blessed shall you be in the city, and blessed shall you be in the country. Blessed shall be the fruit of your body, the produce of your ground and the increase of your herds, the increase of your cattle and the offspring of your flocks. Blessed shall be your basket and your kneading bowl. Blessed shall you be when you come in, and blessed shall you be when you go out. The LORD will cause your enemies who rise against you to be defeated before your face; they shall come out against you one way and flee before you seven ways. The LORD will command the blessing on you in your storehouses and in all to which you set your hand, and He will bless you in the land which the LORD your God is giving you." *Deuteronomy 28:2–8*

And the LORD will grant you plenty of goods, in the fruit of your body, in the increase of your livestock, and in the produce of your ground, in the land of which the LORD swore to your fathers to give you. The LORD will open to you His good treasure, the heavens, to give the rain to your land in its season, and to bless all the work of your hand. You shall lend to many nations, but you shall not borrow. And the LORD will make you the head and not the tail; you shall be above only, and not be beneath, if you heed the commandments of the LORD your God, which I command you today, and are careful to observe them.

Deuteronomy 28:11–13

"Give, and it will be given to you: good measure, pressed down, shaken together, and running over will be put into your bosom. For with the same measure that you use, it will be measured back to you." *Luke 6:38*

"Heal the sick, cleanse the lepers, raise the dead, cast out demons. Freely you have received, freely give."

Matthew 10:8

"Bring all the tithes into the storehouse, that there may be food in My house, and try Me now in this," says the LORD of hosts, "If I will not open for you the windows of heaven and pour out for you such blessing that there will not be room enough to receive it. And I will rebuke the devourer for your sakes, so that he will not destroy the fruit of your ground, nor shall the vine fail to bear fruit for you in the field," says the LORD of hosts; "And all nations will call you blessed, for you will be a delightful land," says the LORD of hosts. *Malachi 3:10–12*

On the first day of the week let each one of you lay something aside, storing up as he may prosper, that there be no collections when I come.   *1 Corinthians 16:2*

But this I say: He who sows sparingly will also reap sparingly, and he who sows bountifully will also reap bountifully. So let each one give as he purposes in his heart, not grudgingly or of necessity; for God loves a cheerful giver. And God is able to make all grace abound toward you, that you, always having all sufficiency in all things, may have an abundance for every good work.   *2 Corinthians 9:6–8*

"And everyone who has left houses or brothers or sisters or father or mother or wife or children or lands, for My name's sake, shall receive a hundredfold, and inherit eternal life."   *Matthew 19:29*

This Book of the Law shall not depart from your mouth, but you shall meditate in it day and night, that you may observe to do according to all that is written in it. For then you will make your way prosperous, and then you will have good success.   *Joshua 1:8*

For God gives wisdom and knowledge and joy to a man who is good in His sight; but to the sinner He gives the work of gathering and collecting, that he may give to him who is good before God. This also is vanity and grasping for the wind.   *Ecclesiastes 2:26*

A good man leaves an inheritance to his children's children, but the wealth of the sinner is stored up for the righteous.   *Proverbs 13:22*

For the L ORD your God is bringing you into a good land, a land of brooks of water, of fountains and springs, that flow out of valleys and hills; A land of wheat and barley, of vines and fig trees and pomegranates, a land of olive oil and honey; a land in which you will eat bread without scarcity, in which you will lack nothing; a land whose stones are iron and out of whose hills you can dig copper. When you have eaten and are full, then you shall bless the L ORD your God for the good land which He has given you. Beware that you do not forget the L ORD your God by not keeping His commandments, His judgments, and His statutes which I command you today, lest—when you have eaten and are full, and have built beautiful houses and dwell in them; Aad when your herds and your flocks multiply, and your silver and your gold are multiplied, and all that you have is multiplied; when your heart is lifted up, and you forget the L ORD your God who brought you out of the land of Egypt, from the house of bondage. . . . And you shall remember the L ORD your God, for it is He who gives you power to get wealth, that He may establish His covenant which He swore to your fathers, as it is this day.
Deuteronomy 8:7–14, 18

"Therefore do not worry, saying, 'What shall we eat?' or 'What shall we drink?' or 'What shall we wear?' For after all these things the Gentiles seek. For your heavenly Father knows that you need all these things. But seek first the kingdom of God and His righteousness, and all these things shall be added to you."   *Matthew 6:31–33*

And my God shall supply all your need according to His riches in glory by Christ Jesus.   *Philippians 4:19*

WHAT TO DO WHEN—You Are Having Marital Problems.

And the LORD God said, "It is not good that man should be alone; I will make him a helper comparable to him."
Genesis 2:18

Submitting to one another in the fear of God. Wives, submit to your own husbands, as to the Lord. For the husband is head of the wife, as also Christ is head of the church; and He is the Savior of the body. Therefore, just as the church is subject to Christ, so let the wives be to their own husbands in everything. Husbands, love your wives, just as Christ also loved the church and gave Himself for her, that He might sanctify and cleanse her with the washing of water by the word, that He might present her to Himself a glorious church, not having spot or wrinkle or any such thing, but that she should be holy and without blemish. So husbands ought to love their own wives as their own bodies; he who loves his wife loves himself. For no one ever hated his own flesh, but nourishes and cherishes it, just as the Lord does the church. For we are members of His body, of His flesh and of His bones. "For this reason a man shall leave his father and mother and be joined to his wife, and the two shall become one flesh." This is a great mystery, but I speak concerning Christ and the church. Nevertheless let each one of you in particular so love his own wife as himself, and let the wife see that she respects her husband.   *Ephesians 5:21–33*

Let all bitterness, wrath, anger, clamor, and evil speaking be put away from you, with all malice. And be kind to one another, tenderhearted, forgiving one another, even as God in Christ forgave you.   *Ephesians 4:31–32*

Therefore a man shall leave his father and mother and be joined to his wife, and they shall become one flesh.
Genesis 2:24

Wives, likewise, be submissive to your own husbands, that even if some do not obey the word, they, without a word, may be won by the conduct of their wives, when they observe your chaste conduct accompanied by fear. Do not let your adornment be merely outward—arranging the hair, wearing gold, or putting on fine apparel—rather let it be the hidden person of the heart, with the incorruptible beauty of a gentle and quiet spirit, which is very precious in the sight of God. For in this manner, in former times, the holy women who trusted in God also adorned themselves, being submissive to their own husbands, as Sarah obeyed Abraham, calling him lord, whose daughters you are if you do good and are not afraid with any terror. Husbands, likewise, dwell with them with understanding, giving honor to the wife, as to the weaker vessel, and as being heirs together of the grace of life, that your prayers may not be hindered.   *1 Peter 3:1–7*

Trust in the Lord with all your heart, and lean not on your own understanding; in all your ways acknowledge Him, and He shall direct your paths.   *Proverbs 3:5–6*

And if it seems evil to you to serve the L ORD, choose for yourselves this day whom you will serve, whether the gods which your fathers served that were on the other side of the River, or the gods of the Amorites, in whose land you dwell. But as for me and my house, we will serve the L ORD.

Joshua 24:15

Love does no harm to a neighbor; therefore love is the fulfillment of the law.

Romans 13:10

I will behave wisely in a perfect way. Oh, when will You come to me? I will walk within my house with a perfect heart.

Psalm 101:2

Finally, all of you be of one mind, having compassion for one another; love as brothers, be tenderhearted, be courteous; not returning evil for evil or reviling for reviling, but on the contrary blessing, knowing that you were called to this, that you may inherit a blessing. For "he who would love life and see good days, let him refrain his tongue from evil, and his lips from speaking deceit. Let him turn away from evil and do good; let him seek peace and pursue it."

1 Peter 3:8–11

Hatred stirs up strife, but love covers all sins.

Proverbs 10:12

Since you have purified your souls in obeying the truth through the Spirit in sincere love of the brethren, love one another fervently with a pure heart.

1 Peter 1:22

WHAT TO DO WHEN—Waiting on God.

Wait on the LORD; be of good courage, and He shall strengthen your heart; wait, I say, on the LORD!
Psalm 27:14

My soul, wait silently for God alone, for my expectation is from Him.
Psalm 62:5

Our soul waits for the LORD; He is our help and our shield.
Psalm 33:20

But those who wait on the LORD shall renew their strength; they shall mount up with wings like eagles, they shall run and not be weary, they shall walk and not faint.
Isaiah 40:31

For the vision is yet for an appointed time; but at the end it will speak, and it will not lie. Though it tarries, wait for it; because it will surely come, it will not tarry.
Habakkuk 2:3

Let us hold fast the confession of our hope without wavering, for He who promised is faithful.   *Hebrews 10:23*

The eyes of all look expectantly to You, and You give them their food in due season. You open Your hand and satisfy the desire of every living thing.   *Psalm 145:15–16*

I wait for the LORD, my soul waits, and in His word I do hope.
Psalm 130:5

For we have become partakers of Christ if we hold the beginning of our confidence steadfast to the end.
Hebrews 3:14

And it will be said in that day: "Behold, this is our God; we have waited for Him, and He will save us. This is the LORD; we have waited for Him; we will be glad and rejoice in His salvation."
Isaiah 25:9

WHAT THE BIBLE HAS TO SAY ABOUT—Faith.

Now faith is the substance of things hoped for, the evidence of things not seen.
Hebrews 11:1

So then faith comes by hearing, and hearing by the word of God.
Romans 10:17

For I say, through the grace given to me, to everyone who is among you, not to think of himself more highly than he ought to think, but to think soberly, as God has dealt to each one a measure of faith.
Romans 12:3

Looking unto Jesus, the author and finisher of our faith, who for the joy that was set before Him endured the cross, despising the shame, and has sat down at the right hand of the throne of God.
Hebrews 12:2

So Jesus said to them, "Because of your unbelief; for assuredly, I say to you, if you have faith as a mustard seed, you will say to this mountain, 'Move from here to there,' and it will move; and nothing will be impossible for you."
Matthew 17:20

So Jesus answered and said to them, "Have faith in God. For assuredly, I say to you, whoever says to this mountain, 'Be removed and be cast into the sea,' and does not doubt in his heart, but believes that those things he says will be done, he will have whatever he says. Therefore I say to you, whatever things you ask when you pray, believe that you receive them, and you will have them."   *Mark 11:22–24*

For in it the righteousness of God is revealed from faith to faith; as it is written, "The just shall live by faith."
Romans 1:17

For we walk by faith, not by sight.   *2 Corinthians 5:7*

But without faith it is impossible to please Him, for he who comes to God must believe that He is, and that He is a rewarder of those who diligently seek Him.   *Hebrews 11:6*

That the genuineness of your faith, being much more precious than gold that perishes, though it is tested by fire, may be found to praise, honor, and glory at the revelation of Jesus Christ, whom having not seen you love. Though now you do not see Him, yet believing, you rejoice with joy inexpressible and full of glory, receiving the end of your faith—the salvation of your souls.   *1 Peter 1:7–9*

For whatever is born of God overcomes the world. And this is the victory that has overcome the world—our faith.
1 John 5:4

And suddenly, a woman who had a flow of blood for twelve years came from behind and touched the hem of His garment. For she said to herself, "If only I may touch His garment, I shall be made well." But Jesus turned around, and when He saw her He said, "be of good cheer, daughter; your faith has made you well." And the woman was made well from that hour. *Matthew 9:20–22*

And when He had come into the house, the blind men came to Him. And Jesus said to them, "Do you believe that I am able to do this?" They said to Him, "Yes, Lord." Then He touched their eyes, saying, "According to your faith let it be to you." *Matthew 9:28–29*

Jesus said to him, "If you can believe, all things are possible to him who believes." *Mark 9:23*

Is anyone among you sick? Let him call for the elders of the church, and let them pray over him, anointing him with oil in the name of the Lord. And the prayer of faith will save the sick, and the Lord will raise him up.
James 5:14–15

WHAT THE BIBLE HAS TO SAY ABOUT—Serving God.

"No one can serve two masters; for either he will hate the one and love the other, or else he will be loyal to the one and despise the other. You cannot serve God and mammon." *Matthew 6:24*

You shall walk after the Lord your God and fear Him, and keep His commandments and obey His voice; you shall serve Him and hold fast to Him.   *Deuteronomy 13:4*

Then Jesus said to him, "Away with you, Satan! For it is written, 'You shall worship the Lord your God, and Him only you shall serve.'"   *Matthew 4:10*

But take careful heed to do the commandment and the law which Moses the servant of the Lord commanded you, to love the Lord your God, to walk in all His ways, to keep His commandments, to hold fast to Him, and to serve Him with all your heart and with all your soul.   *Joshua 22:5*

I beseech you therefore, brethren, by the mercies of God, that you present your bodies a living sacrifice, holy, acceptable to God, which is your reasonable service. And do not be conformed to this world, but be transformed by the renewing of your mind, that you may prove what is that good and acceptable and perfect will of God.
Romans 12:1–2

Be kindly affectionate to one another with brotherly love, in honor giving preference to one another; not lagging in diligence, fervent in spirit, serving the Lord … distributing to the needs of the saints, given to hospitality.
Romans 12:10–11, 13

But now we have been delivered from the law, having died to what we were held by, so that we should serve in the newness of the Spirit and not in the oldness of the letter.   *Romans 7:6*

So you shall serve the L ORD your God, and He will bless your bread and your water. And I will take sickness away from the midst of you. No one shall suffer miscarriage or be barren in your land; I will fulfill the number of your days.   *Exodus 23:25–26*

And it shall be that if you earnestly obey My commandments which I command you today, to love the L ORD your God and serve Him with all your heart and with all your soul, then I will give you the rain for your land in its season, the early rain and the latter rain, that you may gather in your grain, your new wine, and your oil. And I will send grass in your fields for your livestock, that you may eat and be filled.   *Deuteronomy 11:13–15*

And if it seems evil to you to serve the L ORD, choose for yourselves this day whom you will serve, whether the gods which your fathers served that were on the other side of the River, or the gods of the Amorites, in whose land you dwell. But as for me and my house, we will serve the L ORD.   *Joshua 24:15*

Then Samuel said to the people, "Do not fear. You have done all this wickedness; yet do not turn aside from following the Lord, but serve the L ORD with all your heart. And do not turn aside; for then you would go after empty things which cannot profit or deliver, for they are nothing. For the L ORD will not forsake His people, for His great name's sake, because it has pleased the L ORD to make you His people."   *1 Samuel 12:20–22*

And now, Israel, what does the LORD your God require of you, but to fear the LORD your God, to walk in all His ways and to love Him, to serve the LORD your God with all your heart and with all your soul.   *Deuteronomy 10:12*

As for you, my son Solomon, know the God of your father, and serve Him with a loyal heart and with a willing mind; for the LORD searches all hearts and understands all the intent of the thoughts. If you seek Him, He will be found by you; but if you forsake Him, He will cast you off forever.   *1 Chronicles 28:9*

Make a joyful shout to the LORD, all you lands! Serve the LORD with gladness; come before His presence with singing. . . . Enter into His gates with thanksgiving, and into His courts with praise. Be thankful to Him, and bless His name.   *Psalm 100:1–2, 4*

WHAT THE BIBLE HAS TO SAY ABOUT—the Grace of God.

And with great power the apostles gave witness to the resurrection of the Lord Jesus. And great grace was upon them all.   *Acts 4:33*

And so find favor and high esteem in the sight of God and man.   *Proverbs 3:4*

For the LORD God is a sun and shield; the LORD will give grace and glory; no good thing will He withhold from those who walk uprightly.   *Psalm 84:11*

So the LORD said to Moses, "I will also do this thing that you have spoken; for you have found grace in My sight, and I know you by name."   *Exodus 33:17*

You have granted me life and favor, and Your care has preserved my spirit.   *Job 10:12*

For You, O LORD, will bless the righteous; with favor You will surround him as with a shield.   *Psalm 5:12*

LORD, by Your favor You have made my mountain stand strong; you hid Your face, and I was troubled.   *Psalm 30:7*

The LORD has been mindful of us; He will bless us; He will bless the house of Israel; He will bless the house of Aaron. He will bless those who fear the LORD, both small and great.   *Psalm 115:12–13*

For whoever finds me finds life, and obtains favor from the LORD.   *Proverbs 8:35*

Blessings are on the head of the righteous, but violence covers the mouth of the wicked. The blessing of the LORD makes one rich, and He adds no sorrow with it. The fear of the wicked will come upon him, and the desire of the righteous will be granted.   *Proverbs 10:6, 22, 24*

Fools mock at sin, but among the upright there is favor.   *Proverbs 14:9*

The sons of foreigners shall build up your walls, and their kings shall minister to you; for in My wrath I struck you, but in My favor I have had mercy on you.

Isaiah 60:10

For all things are for your sakes, that grace, having spread through the many, may cause thanksgiving to abound to the glory of God.   *2 Corinthians 4:15*

To the praise of the glory of His grace, by which He made us accepted in the Beloved.   *Ephesians 1:6*

Let us therefore come boldly to the throne of grace, that we may obtain mercy and find grace to help in time of need.   *Hebrews 4:16*

WHAT THE BIBLE HAS TO SAY ABOUT—the Holy Spirit.

Or do you not know that your body is the temple of the Holy Spirit who is in you, whom you have from God, and you are not your own?   *1 Corinthians 6:19*

Now hope does not disappoint, because the love of God has been poured out in our hearts by the Holy Spirit who was given to us.   *Romans 5:5*

"And I will pray the Father, and He will give you another Helper, that He may abide with you forever—the Spirit of truth, whom the world cannot receive, because it neither sees Him nor knows Him; but you know Him, for He dwells with you and will be in you."   *John 14:16–17*

Nevertheless I tell you the truth. It is to your advantage that I go away; for if I do not go away, the Helper will not come to you; but if I depart, I will send Him to you. . . . However, when He, the Spirit of truth, has come, He will guide you into all truth; for He will not speak on His own authority, but whatever He hears He will speak; and He will tell you things to come.   *John 16:7, 13*

I indeed baptize you with water unto repentance, but He who is coming after me is mightier than I, whose sandals I am not worthy to carry. He will baptize you with the Holy Spirit and fire.   *Matthew 3:11*

"If you then, being evil, know how to give good gifts to your children, how much more will your heavenly Father give the Holy Spirit to those who ask Him!"   *Luke 11:13*

And it shall come to pass afterward that I will pour out My Spirit on all flesh; your sons and your daughters shall prophesy, your old men shall dream dreams, your young men shall see visions.   *Joel 2:28*

And being assembled together with them, He commanded them not to depart from Jerusalem, but to wait for the Promise of the Father, "which," He said, "you have heard from Me; for John truly baptized with water, but you shall be baptized with the Holy Spirit not many days from now. . . . But you shall receive power when the Holy Spirit has come upon you; and you shall be witnesses to Me in Jerusalem, and in all Judea and Samaria, and to the end of the earth."   *Acts 1:4–5, 8*

"He who believes in Me, as the Scripture has said, out of his heart will flow rivers of living water." But this He spoke concerning the Spirit, whom those believing in Him would receive; for the Holy Spirit was not yet given, because Jesus was not yet glorified.   *John 7:38–39*

And they were all filled with the Holy Spirit and began to speak with other tongues, as the Spirit gave them utterance.   *Acts 2:4*

Then Peter said to them, "Repent, and let every one of you be baptized in the name of Jesus Christ for the remission of sins; and you shall receive the gift of the Holy Spirit."   *Acts 2:38*

And when they had prayed, the place where they were assembled together was shaken; and they were all filled with the Holy Spirit, and they spoke the word of God with boldness.   *Acts 4:31*

And do not be drunk with wine, in which is dissipation; but be filled with the Spirit.   *Ephesians 5:18*

Now when the apostles who were at Jerusalem heard that Samaria had received the word of God, they sent Peter and John to them, who, when they had come down, prayed for them that they might receive the Holy Spirit. For as yet He had fallen upon none of them. They had only been baptized in the name of the Lord Jesus. Then they laid hands on them, and they received the Holy Spirit.
                                             Acts 8:14–17

While Peter was still speaking these words, the Holy Spirit fell upon all those who heard the word. And those of the circumcision who believed were astonished, as many as came with Peter, because the gift of the Holy Spirit had been poured out on the Gentiles also. For they heard them speak with tongues and magnify God.   *Acts 10:44–46*

He said to them, "Did you receive the Holy Spirit when you believed?" So they said to him, "We have not so much as heard whether there is a Holy Spirit." And he said to them, "Into what then were you baptized?" So they said, "Into John's baptism." Then Paul said, "John indeed baptized with a baptism of repentance, saying to the people that they should believe on Him who would come after him, that is, on Christ Jesus." When they heard this, they were baptized in the name of the Lord Jesus. And when Paul had laid hands on them, the Holy Spirit came upon them, and they spoke with tongues and prophesied.   *Acts 19:2–6*

WHAT THE BIBLE HAS TO SAY ABOUT—God's Faithfulness.

He who calls you is faithful, who also will do it.
                                        1 Thessalonians 5:24

"For this is like the waters of Noah to Me; for as I have sworn that the waters of Noah would no longer cover the earth, so have I sworn that I would not be angry with you, nor rebuke you. For the mountains shall depart and the hills be removed, but My kindness shall not depart from you, nor shall My covenant of peace be removed," says the LORD, who has mercy on you.   *Isaiah 54:9–10*

You have dealt well with Your servant, O Lord, according to Your word.   *Psalm 119:65*

The rainbow shall be in the cloud, and I will look on it to remember the everlasting covenant between God and every living creature of all flesh that is on the earth.
                                                        Genesis 9:16

Behold, I am with you and will keep you wherever you go, and will bring you back to this land; for I will not leave you until I have done what I have spoken to you.
                                                       Genesis 28:15

But because the Lord loves you, and because He would keep the oath which He swore to your fathers, the Lord has brought you out with a mighty hand, and redeemed you from the house of bondage, from the hand of Pharaoh king of Egypt. Therefore know that the Lord your God, He is God, the faithful God who keeps covenant and mercy for a thousand generations with those who love Him and keep His commandments.   *Deuteronomy 7:8–9*

Behold, this day I am going the way of all the earth. And you know in all your hearts and in all your souls that not one thing has failed of all the good things which the Lord your God spoke concerning you. All have come to pass for you; not one word of them has failed. *Joshua 23:14*

Blessed be the Lord, who has given rest to His people Israel, according to all that He promised. There has not failed one word of all His good promise, which He promised through His servant Moses.   *1 Kings 8:56*

Your mercy, O Lord, is in the heavens; Your faithfulness reaches to the clouds. *Psalm 36:5*

I will sing of the mercies of the Lord forever; with my mouth will I make known Your faithfulness to all generations. For I have said, "Mercy shall be built up forever; Your faithfulness You shall establish in the very heavens." . . . Nevertheless My lovingkindness I will not utterly take from him, nor allow My faithfulness to fail. My covenant I will not break, nor alter the word that has gone out of My lips. *Psalm 89:1–2, 33–34*

He will not allow your foot to be moved; he who keeps you will not slumber. Behold, he who keeps Israel shall neither slumber nor sleep. *Psalm 121:3–4*

God is faithful, by whom you were called into the fellowship of His Son, Jesus Christ our Lord.
1 Corinthians 1:9

No temptation has overtaken you except such as is common to man; but God is faithful, who will not allow you to be tempted beyond what you are able, but with the temptation will also make the way of escape, that you may be able to bear it. *1 Corinthians 10:13*

The Lord is not slack concerning His promise, as some count slackness, but is longsuffering toward us, not willing that any should perish but that all should come to repentance. *2 Peter 3:9*

If we are faithless, He remains faithful; He cannot deny Himself. Nevertheless the solid foundation of God stands, having this seal: "The Lord knows those who are His," and, "Let everyone who names the name of Christ depart from iniquity."   *2 Timothy 2:13, 19*

WHAT THE BIBLE HAS TO SAY ABOUT—the Church.

That in the dispensation of the fullness of the times He might gather together in one all things in Christ, both which are in heaven and which are on earth—in Him.... And He put all things under His feet, and gave Him to be head over all things to the church, which is His body, the fullness of Him who fills all in all.   *Ephesians 1:10, 22–23*

He has delivered us from the power of darkness and conveyed us into the kingdom of the Son of His love.... And He is the head of the body, the church, who is the beginning, the firstborn from the dead, that in all things He may have the preeminence.   *Colossians 1:13, 18*

He said to them, "But who do you say that I am?" Simon Peter answered and said, "You are the Christ, the Son of the living God." Jesus answered and said to him, "Blessed are you, Simon Bar-Jonah, for flesh and blood has not revealed this to you, but My Father who is in heaven. And I also say to you that you are Peter, and on this rock I will build My church, and the gates of Hades shall not prevail against it."   *Matthew 16:15–18*

Having been built on the foundation of the apostles and prophets, Jesus Christ Himself being the chief cornerstone, in whom the whole building, being fitted together, grows into a holy temple in the Lord, in whom you also are being built together for a dwelling place of God in the Spirit.

Ephesians 2:20–22

From whom the whole family in heaven and earth is named.... To Him be glory in the church by Christ Jesus to all generations, forever and ever. Amen.

Ephesians 3:15, 21

For the husband is head of the wife, as also Christ is head of the church; and He is the Savior of the body. Therefore, just as the church is subject to Christ, so let the wives be to their own husbands in everything. Husbands, love your wives, just as Christ also loved the church and gave Himself for her, that He might sanctify and cleanse her with the washing of water by the word, that He might present her to Himself a glorious church, not having spot or wrinkle or any such thing, but that she should be holy and without blemish.... For no one ever hated his own flesh, but nourishes and cherishes it, just as the Lord does the church.

Ephesians 5:23–27, 29

And you are complete in Him, who is the head of all principality and power.... And not holding fast to the Head, from whom all the body, nourished and knit together by joints and ligaments, grows with the increase that is from God.

Colossians 2:10, 19

For as we have many members in one body, but all the members do not have the same function, so we, being many, are one body in Christ, and individually members of one another.

Romans 12:4–5

For as the body is one and has many members, but all the members of that one body, being many, are one body, so also is Christ. For by one Spirit we were all baptized into one body—whether Jews or Greeks, whether slaves or free—and have all been made to drink into one Spirit. For in fact the body is not one member but many. If the foot should say, "Because I am not a hand, I am not of the body," is it therefore not of the body? And if the ear should say, "Because I am not an eye, I am not of the body," is it therefore not of the body? If the whole body were an eye, where would be the hearing? If the whole were hearing, where would be the smelling? But now God has set the members, each one of them, in the body just as He pleased. And if they were all one member, where would the body be? But now indeed there are many members, yet one body. And the eye cannot say to the hand, "I have no need of you"; nor again the head to the feet, "I have no need of you." No, much rather, those members of the body which seem to be weaker are necessary. And those members of the body which we think to be less honorable, on these we bestow greater honor; and our unpresentable parts have greater modesty, But our presentable parts have no need. But God composed the body, having given greater honor to that part which lacks it, that there should be no schism in the body, but that the members should have the same care for one another. And if one member suffers, all the members suffer with it; or if one member is honored, all the members rejoice with it. Now you are the body of Christ, and members individually. And God has appointed these in the church: first apostles, second prophets, third teachers, after that miracles, then gifts of healings, helps, administrations, varieties of tongues.

1 Corinthians 12:12–28

And we urge you, brethren, to recognize those who labor among you, and are over you in the Lord and admonish you, and to esteem them very highly in love for their work's sake. Be at peace among yourselves.

1 Thessalonians 5:12–13

And He Himself gave some to be apostles, some prophets, some evangelists, and some pastors and teachers, for the equipping of the saints for the work of ministry, for the edifying of the body of Christ. *Ephesians 4:11–12*

Then those who gladly received his word were baptized; and that day about three thousand souls were added to them. And they continued steadfastly in the apostles' doctrine and fellowship, in the breaking of bread, and in prayers. Then fear came upon every soul, and many wonders and signs were done through the apostles. Now all who believed were together, and had all things in common, and sold their possessions and goods, and divided them among all, as anyone had need. So continuing daily with one accord in the temple, and breaking bread from house to house, they ate their food with gladness and simplicity of heart, praising God and having favor with all the people. And the Lord added to the church daily those who were being saved. *Acts 2:41–47*

Remember those who rule over you, who have spoken the word of God to you, whose faith follow, considering the outcome of their conduct.... Obey those who rule over you, and be submissive, for they watch out for your souls, as those who must give account. Let them do so with joy and not with grief, for that would be unprofitable for you.

Hebrews 13:7, 17

Behold, how good and how pleasant it is for brethren to dwell together in unity!   *Psalm 133:1*

✑ PRAYER LIST FOR SOULS ✑

PRAYER LIST FOR SOULS

PRAYER LIST FOR SOULS

PRAYER LIST FOR SOULS

PRAYER LIST FOR SOULS

SOULS WON FOR CHRIST

SOULS WON FOR CHRIST

SOULS WON FOR CHRIST

SOULS WON FOR CHRIST

SOULS WON FOR CHRIST

❧ SOULS WON FOR CHRIST ❧

SOULS WON FOR CHRIST

SOULS WON FOR CHRIST

SOULS WON FOR CHRIST

❧ SOULS WON FOR CHRIST ❧